Integrating Study Abroad
into the Undergraduate
Liberal Arts Curriculum

Recent Titles in
Contributions to the Study of Education

Improving Educational Quality: A Global Perspective
David W. Chapman and Carol A. Carrier, editors

Rethinking the Curriculum: Toward an Integrated, Interdisciplinary
College Education
Mary E. Clark and Sandra A. Wawrytko, editors

Study Abroad: The Experience of American Undergraduates
Jerry S. Carlson, Barbara B. Burn, John Useem, and David Yachimowicz

Between Understanding and Misunderstanding: Problems and Prospects
for International Cultural Exchange
Yasushi Sugiyama, editor

Southern Cities, Southern Schools: Public Education in the Urban South
David N. Plank and Rick Ginsberg, editors

Making Schools Work for Underachieving Minority Students: Next Steps
for Research, Policy, and Practice
Josie G. Bain and Joan L. Herman, editors

Foreign Teachers in China: Old Problems for a New Generation, 1979-1989
Edgar A. Porter

Effective Interventions: Applying Learning Theory to School Social Work
Evelyn Harris Ginsburg

Cognitive Education and Testing: A Methodological Approach
Eugene J. Meehan

American Presidents and Education
Maurice R. Berube

Learning to Lead: The Dynamics of the High School Principalship
Gordon A. Donaldson, Jr.

Windows on Japanese Education
Edward R. Beauchamp, editor

Integrating Study Abroad into the Undergraduate Liberal Arts Curriculum

Eight Institutional Case Studies

Edited by
BARBARA B. BURN

Contributions to the Study of Education, Number 44

GREENWOOD PRESS
New York • Westport, Connecticut • London

Library of Congress Cataloging-in-Publication Data

Integrating study abroad into the undergraduate liberal arts
  curriculum : eight institutional case studies / edited by Barbara B.
  Burn.
      p.   cm.—(Contributions to the study of education, ISSN
  0196-707X ; no. 44)
    Includes bibliographical references and index.
    ISBN 0-313-27780-X (alk. paper)
      1. Foreign study—Case studies.   2. American students—Foreign
  countries—Case studies.   I. Burn, Barbara B.   II. Series.
  LB2375.I53   1991
  370.19′6—dc20   90-22620

British Library Cataloguing in Publication Data is available.

Library of Congress Catalog Card Number: 90-22620
ISBN: 0-313-27780-X
ISSN: 0196-707X

First published in 1991

Greenwood Press, 88 Post Road West, Westport, CT 06881
An imprint of Greenwood Publishing Group, Inc.

Printed in the United States of America

The paper used in this book complies with the
Permanent Paper Standard issued by the National
Information Standards Organization (Z39.48-1984).

10 9 8 7 6 5 4 3 2 1

CONTENTS

THE STUDY ABROAD ARTICULATION PROJECT: INTRODUCTION

Barbara B. Burn

The eight case studies presented in this volume describe activities undertaken in as many colleges and universities as part of what was called the Study Abroad Articulation Project (SAAP). It had as its overall objectives (1) to identify factors, circumstances, and attitudes that prevent study abroad by American undergraduates from being an important and integral part of their total degree program or for some even excluded by it prevent participation in such programs, and (2) to identify and encourage institutional strategies and policies aimed at eliminating or at least reducing these obstacles. The underlying aim of the project was to strengthen international studies and the internationalization of undergraduate education in the United States by making study abroad more important to and recognized within it.

The Articulation Project was launched in January 1987. It concluded with a two-day workshop held in Amherst, Massachusetts in February 1989. At the workshop the issues raised by the eight SAAP institutions were presented and discussed with project consultants and with the two-person teams sent by eight additional colleges and universities. These institutions were invited to send representatives because of their known commitment to and experience with the integration of study abroad into undergraduate students' degree programs. Appendix I lists the eight original SAAP institutions, the additional eight participating in the February 1989 workshop, and project consultants.

The Study Abroad Articulation Project grew out of an earlier research undertaking, the so-called Study Abroad Evaluation Project (SAEP), especially certain findings of the latter project. The first paper in this volume, written by the chief researcher for the SAEP, Professor Jerry S. Carlson of the University of California at Riverside, highlights aspects of the U.S. involvement in this major five-country, five-year undertaking.

Those most pertinent to the Articulation Project were the following:

- Important deterrents to study abroad by American undergraduates are their impressions that it would be in addition to, not part of, their degree programs and would prolong their degree studies — and even cost more.
- Faculty members not only are rarely a source of information and encouragement for undergraduate study abroad but tend to discourage it, especially undergraduates' taking courses abroad to meet major requirements.
- Returning study abroad students often experience not only difficulty in receiving recognition for academic studies done abroad but little encouragement by the home institution for the experience to be viewed as an important part of their education and a resource for internationalizing their own and other students' college experience.

Perhaps the label applied now for some years to the phenomenon of American undergraduates studying abroad, the "junior year abroad," well captures much of the problem of non-articulation or non-integration of study abroad for American undergraduates. The junior year label connotes a lack of academic seriousness to those only partly familiar with the U.S. system of labeling the four undergraduate years. The early history of study abroad by undergraduates from the United States, starting in the early 1920s with Delaware University and Smith College, wrongfully suggests that the experience was for "Grand Tour" kinds of aims rather than something more lasting and significant. From this early stage when in fact study abroad for female students was highly professional in aim, it being important in preparing women for one of the few careers then accessible to them—teaching foreign languages—study abroad acquired an image that combined the notions of preciousness, privacy, and non-professional goals.

That this image is obsolete in relation to contemporary career opportunities opening up to American students in not sufficiently appreciated. Moreover, it is not at all well enough understood in the United States that for the emerging generation of college graduates internationally involved careers are not only likely but probable. Except for a few graduate schools of business that give major priority to international education and work experience, such as the University of North Carolina and Pennsylvania State schools of business, very few educational institutions promote international education and experience as indispensable, even quite important, to career paths in most fields.

In this respect the experience of Western Europe, most notably the European Community (EC), is in strong contrast to that of the United States. The ERASMUS Program of the EC (Expanded Regional Action Scheme for the Mobility of University Students) that was launched in 1987 not only aims at a vastly increased level of student exchanges among the EC countries. Most relevant to the Study Abroad Articulation Project, it embraces this as a way to internationalize students' undergraduate programs by encouraging them to pursue course work abroad that falls in their major field and is an important part of their degree program.

A comparison between U.S. study abroad and that under ERASMUS drives home the dramatic differences between them. The great majority of U.S. study abroad students are in the humanities and social science fields; very few are in such professional fields as business and engineering. Moreover, most U.S. students take courses in their so-called electives while on study abroad, that is, courses in which their major department is apt to have little interest. By contrast, under ERASMUS the majority of students studying abroad are in professional fields. Overwhelmingly they are in law, business, engineering, and the sciences. Most important, while abroad they are taking courses in their major field. European Community students abroad under ERASMUS do not spend time studying foreign cultures but focus on professionally relevant subjects in their specializations. The foregoing comments should amply suggest the relative importance attributed to the study abroad experience by European and U.S. professors if American students are encouraged mainly to take courses that are not part of their major.

The Articulation Project was fortunate in obtaining funding from the Ford Foundation. This support gave an important imprimatur to the project, which reenforced its value to the international studies field and to American higher education. Because an important concern of the foundation in funding the project was to encourage more internationalization of the undergraduate liberal arts curriculum, the foundation's support influenced in part the identification of some of the institutions participating in the project.

The initial four institutions were those that had participated in the earlier five-country Study Abroad Evaluation Project: the University of Colorado at Boulder, the University of California, Kalamazoo College, and, the U.S. coordinating institution for the SAEP, the University of Massachusetts at Amherst. The other four SAAP institutions, all strong in undergraduate liberal arts, were Pomona, Earlham, and Smith Colleges, and Georgetown University.

At each of these eight institutions the issue of making study abroad an integral part of students' undergraduate programs was perceived somewhat differently. Each institution had its own focus in deciding on its activities and carrying them out under the Study Abroad Articulation Project. They ranged from concerns with inadequate faculty support, to disjunctions between the U.S. and European higher education systems, to needs for more follow-up and reenforcement of foreign language skills for study abroad returnees, to the need for faculty to recognize and build on the experience abroad of these returnees in curriculum development and implementation. These and related issues are increasingly recognized as of growing importance to the whole field of study abroad and to its contribution to international education.

Integrating Study Abroad into the Undergraduate Liberal Arts Curriculum

RELEVANT RESULTS FROM THE STUDY ABROAD ARTICULATION PROJECT

Jerry S. Carlson

The Study Abroad Evaluation Project (SAEP) was undertaken to examine in detail student exchange between selected countries within the European Community and between these countries and four institutions of higher learning in the United States.[1] The European countries involved in the project were the Federal Republic of Germany, France, Sweden, and the United Kingdom. The participating American institutions were the University of California, the University of Colorado, Kalamazoo College, and the coordinating institution for the United States, the University of Massachusetts at Amherst. The research involved the analysis of home and host institution programs and curricula as well as study of the impacts that foreign study has on participating students.

Four research questions guided the student impact part of the U.S. involvement in the project SAEP:

1. Who chooses to study abroad? Or, how do those students who study abroad differ from students sharing similar characteristics who remain on their home campuses?

2. What changes occur in the two groups of students over the course of the junior year?

3. What aspects of the individual and/or the sojourn abroad contribute to variation in the changes observed?

4. What are the long-term effects of the study abroad experience? How pervasive and durable are they?

In order to address these questions, a longitudinal, comparison group, pre-measure post-measure research design was employed. Some 250 sophomores who had been selected to study abroad in their junior year comprised the study abroad group; sophomores who had equivalent grade point averages as the study abroad group but who had not chosen to study abroad constituted the comparison group. Questionnaires were used to gather information on the first three research questions of the study. The fourth research question was approached by using focused interview techniques with individuals who had participated in study abroad between five and twenty years ago.

The pre-junior year questionnaires obtained information on the following areas:

a. Background and demographic information

    level of education and occupation of mother and father

    reasons for choosing the home institution

    financing of education

    GPA and self-evaluation of academic strength

b. Foreign interest and experience

c. Knowledge of and attitudes toward the United States and foreign countries

d. Learning styles and attitudes toward home institution (does emphasize-should emphasize)

e. Career goals and/or orientations

f. Foreign language proficiency

g. Motivation, choice and preparation for study abroad

The post-junior year questionnaires focused on:

a. Many of the same questions asked in the pre-junior year questionnaires, allowing comparisons between the pre-junior year and post-junior year measures

b. Living accommodations while abroad

c. Academic life and satisfaction while abroad, including comparisons and critiques of home and host institutions

d. Personal activities and development while abroad

e. Language

f. The relationship of study abroad to academic programs at home

g. Value of study abroad personally, academically, and with regard to future career or profession

PRIOR TO THE SOJOURN

Academic Issues

The academic majors of the study abroad students varied substantially from those of the comparison group. The study abroad students tended to major in the humanities and social sciences, business, and education (81% of the majors were in these areas). Only 19% of this group majored in the sciences or mathematics. The comparison group was representative of the University of California and University of Massachusetts at Amherst undergraduate sophomore populations: 60% majored in the humanities, social sciences, business, and eduction; 40% majored in the sciences, mathematics, and engineering.

The reasons that the students from both the study abroad and comparison groups gave for choosing their majors were similar. The most highly rated factor was interest and perceived ability to succeed in the subject matter. Career and job related factors were somewhat less important, although the comparison group ranked career as more important for their choice of major than did the study abroad students. This is consistent with another finding of the project: the study abroad students were less set in their career aspirations than the comparison group students.

The study abroad students were asked when they were informed about the study abroad programs at their college or university. Approximately 50% of the students reported that they had been informed about study abroad prior to entering college. At Kalamazoo College, 96% of those queried reported that they knew of study abroad prior to enrolling.

When asked if information about study abroad was part of general information related to the field of study in which the student was interested, 81% of the Kalamazoo students responded positively; less than 30% of the students from the other U.S. universities answered this question positively, reporting that the information they received was primarily general in scope, contained in university information packets, and not specific to an academic area.

Student interest in and motivation to actually participate in study abroad came primarily from friends and acquaintances who had been on a study abroad program or from international programs offices. Teaching staffs and student counselors played a minimal role in informing students about the possibility of studying abroad; nor did they motivate them to participate in such a program.

Career Aspects

Study abroad and comparison students were asked to indicate how likely they were to enter postgraduate studies. Both groups averaged just over "2" on a five-point scale, with "1" being most probably and "5" most unlikely. When asked how set they were in their career goals, the study abroad students were less set in their career goals than the comparison students (2.5 for comparison; 3.3 for study abroad).

Reasons to Study Abroad

   Cultural experience, foreign language improvement, desire to live in and make acquaintances from another country, interest in gaining another perspective on their home country, desire for travel, and enhancement of understanding of a particular host country were all ranked as reasons that students gave to study abroad. Ranked just below these was the expectation that the study abroad experience would improve career prospects.   In fact, approximately one-fourth of the study abroad students planned on careers in international business.   Approximately 90% of the study abroad students believed that they would be able to utilize the foreign sojourn in their later professional life.

   Becoming acquainted with subject matter not offered at their home institution was of only moderate importance in the students' decision to study abroad. Ranked least important was the establishment and/or furtherance of ethnic heritage and/or family ties.

   The comparison group students were asked how interested they were in studying abroad: 54% indicated high interest; 23% indicated low interest. When queried about their reasons for not participating in study abroad, 50% of these students indicated that it was not necessary for their course of study, 40% suggested that it would be inappropriate for their majors, and 45% thought that study abroad might delay their graduation. A sizable fraction thought study abroad would cost more, 69% (not necessarily so).

   In short, the primary reasons students gave for choosing to study abroad were related to their desire to experience new cultures and learn the language of the host country. Academic reasons seemed to be of secondary importance unless the study abroad program was integrated into the academic curriculum of the home institution.

   Although a substantial proportion of the comparison group of students indicated high interest in study abroad, for a variety of reasons they did not participate in it. Primary among these was the perceived lack of curricular relevance of study abroad and the perception that study abroad would delay graduation and cost more than the same period of study at the home campus.

DURING AND SUBSEQUENT TO THE SOJOURN

Academic Issues

   Assessment of the quality of the academic experience overseas was made by a series of questions. These ranged from comparisons of the academic standards of the home and host institutions, to perceptions of the academic standards expected of the American students as contrasted with the standards expected of the host country students, to open-ended questions concerning aspects of the home institutions that the students learned to appreciate or to be critical of as a result of the study abroad experience.

Academic standards abroad compared with home. Generally speaking, the student sojourners perceived the academic standards of the host country to be somewhat inferior to the standards of their home institution. For example, when asked to compare on a five-point scale (1 = much lower; 5 = much higher) the standards abroad with those at home, West Germany and France were ranked at 2.25 and 2.37 respectively. Sweden and the United Kingdom were rated "about the same," 3.0 and 3.03, respectively.

Academic expectations of Americans abroad . On a question aimed at assessing the degree to which the American students were integrated into the academic life of their host institution, the student sojourners were asked to compare the expectations that host institution professors had of them with those that they had for host country nationals. The American respondents indicated that somewhat less was expected of them than of host country nationals. Students who studied in the United Kingdom were an exception.

These results, plus the finding that the American students (again, the UK was an exception) felt that they were graded more leniently than host country nationals, suggest that the perception that the academic standards in France and West Germany are lower than the academic standards in the United States is at least partially effected by the apparent differential, that is, less rigorous treatment accorded American students by French and German professors as well as lack of academic integration of the American students into the structure of the host German and French institutions.

A number of questions remain open concerning the problem of integration of the American students into the academic life of the host European institutions, with language competence undoubtedly playing a significant role, as well as areas of disjunction between the American system of higher education and the systems of higher education in Europe. There may be other reasons for the perception of lower academic standards, however. Although complicated and delicate to approach, these issues must be given serious consideration and fully explored. Otherwise, the often stated goal of integration of American study abroad programs into the academic mainstream of host foreign institutions will remain problematic, and so will the integration of foreign study into the academic programs of home institutions.

Reintegration and Satisfaction with Study Abroad

Although only a small minority of the students who studied abroad changed their majors during the year abroad (9% as opposed to 22% for the comparison group), a sizeable minority

(26%) indicated that they had become interested in courses or areas of study that they had not previously considered. Although the American students' academic horizons broadened as a result of studying and living abroad, they reported that about the only follow-up activity to their experience abroad that they did upon returning to their home institution was to complete questionnaires. The overwhelming majority of respondents (72%) indicated that they had not been involved in their institution in any special way as a result of having been abroad.

In conclusion, the data from the Study Abroad Evaluation Project suggest a number of areas of concern that need to be addressed if foreign study is to be effectively articulated with the academic programs of American universities and colleges. These include student selection, evaluation and reevaluation of academic programs and curricula at home and abroad, and continued concern for academic quality. While university-wide and campus study abroad offices can help address these problematic issues, their efforts alone will not be sufficient. In order to achieve the level of articulation required for an "internationalized" university or college, faculty involvement from both the home and host institutions is essential.

NOTE
1. The U.S. involvement in the SAEP is reported in Jerry S. Carlson, Barbara B. Burn, John Useem, and David Yachimowicz. *Study Abroad: The Experience of American Undergraduates.* Westport CT: Greenwood Press, 1990.

2

EARLHAM COLLEGE: CONNECTING OFF-CAMPUS AND ON-CAMPUS LEARNING

Richard T. Jurasek

The faculty at Earlham College has been pleased to participate in the Study Abroad Articulation Project (SAAP) and provide this report on our activities. Participation has been valuable to us because study abroad at our institution has always been strongly supported: over one-half of each Earlham graduating class has a foreign study experience, typically on one of the ten foreign study programs our college operates. With years of experience behind us in designing and operating programs, we began in the 1980s to focus on the far more complicated teaching and learning dimensions of study sojourns abroad: What is learned off-campus? How is it learned? How can we as educators maximize the impact? We have focused on these questions for nearly a decade, and now that we are sanguine about the learning dimensions of our foreign study programs, can turn to the obvious next question: how can we better articulate between what is learned off-campus and what is learned in on-campus classrooms?

WHAT IS LEARNED ON A STUDY SOJOURN ABROAD?

In addressing the need for improved articulation it is essential to first delineate exactly what is learned on a study sojourn abroad. This became for us the fundamental first step. We could not approach home campus faculty and ask them to work with us on the SAAP if we could not describe exactly what it was that we wanted them to articulate more fully into their teaching on campus.

Fortunately our answer to this question was easier than expected to formulate because our International Programs Office and International Education Committee have been hard at work in sharpening our teaching and learning focus on all of the programs we operate. As a result of this work we now systematically teach about the nature of cultural identity and interaction on all of our programs and bring students to reflect on their cultural assumptions, values, and behavior. It is our basic working assumption that all monocultural people initially apprehend the world with a view that is bound and limited. No matter how globally oriented and cosmopolitan we all might think we are, each of us can make real progress in further refining what can be called perspective consciousness and empathetic understanding. The former is an understanding of the forces that shape the way we see ourselves and others and the realization that our view of the world represents the only way of seeing things. The latter is an awareness of the diversity of ideas and practices found in society throughout the world, as well as limited recognition of what the world might look like from the viewpoint of another cultural insider.

We are sure that most study abroad program designers and operators would acknowledge these as valid goals. But it is our experience that few program designers include a systematic attempt to realize such goals. The actual way we organize such experiential and intellectual learning is beyond the scope of this report. In order to describe our articulation discussions and activities, it will suffice to say that the most unique and perhaps the most valuable kind of learning on a study sojourn is the development of intercultural sensitivity, which is made up of the perspective consciousness and empathetic understanding described below. Although intercultural sensitivity may be at the heart of our rationale for foreign study, it is clear that sojourners also benefit from foreign study in terms of the knowledge and skills they acquire.

A catalog, then, of what is learned at a foreign site includes:

Content learning. During foreign study sojourners typically learn about the history, the art, and the social and political institutions of the host culture. In a few instances, students may also learn about the physical environment at the site: land use patterns, local ecologies, physical geography, and so forth. In many ways, this kind of learning resembles the on-campus emphasis except, of course, that a single locale, country or region is typically treated more thoroughly than in on-campus courses.

Skill development. Typically, one associates improved foreign language skills with study abroad; yet there are others. Students might also develop the skills to conduct biology or geology fieldwork. Students might also develop and use the skills appropriate to the teaching of English as a foreign language. All students generally also develop improved observational skills as a result of their reflective journals and field projects, both of which are required of all students participating in all Earlham College programs.

Intercultural sensitivity. This is made up of the perspective consciousness and empathetic understanding described above. It is difficult to even imagine how such sensitivity can be articulated with the content enrichment and skill development that are typical in on-campus classrooms. It is perhaps easier if we call this learning dimension "perspective training." We can suggest to the faculty that sojourners have learned to distinguish between preconception and the process of perception or that students have been disequilibrized (Piaget) and have begun to explore another culture's epistemology. Sojourners have developed greater cognitive flexibility and a higher tolerance of ambiguity and differentness and relativity. We can tell faculty that returnees are more able to understand, analyze, cope with, and even enjoy the complexities of intercultural interaction. By offering a more differentiated description of intercultural sensitivity, we can suggest to on-campus faculty that the cognitive, perceptual, and intellectual development that they aim for in many of their on-campus courses is very much the core learning event off-campus. So described, it becomes easier for on-campus faculty members to imagine ways they can integrate what is learned abroad into their own teaching agenda on campus.

We have thus discerned content, skills, and intercultural sensitivity as the kinds of learning appropriately associated with study sojourns abroad. Only by describing what is stressed in the off-campus curriculum with as much specificity as possible could we then begin to ask on-campus faculty to imagine ways to improve articulation.

On many campuses foreign study is perceived as a somewhat haphazard but nevertheless valuable learning event that takes place somewhere else, at remote extensions of the home curriculum in France, Japan, or Colombia. Only foreign language learning is a familiar and reliable fix point for homecampus faculty members when they try to imagine what is learned on foreign study. In order to strive for something like a seamless learning continuum that weaves off-campus learning into the overall undergraduate experience, articulators are urged to be as specific as possible when talking about "what should be meshed with what." If we press our on-campus colleagues to improve articulation, we may identify a number of the faculty members who are willing to build new bridges between the distant and the home campus, but there will be very little traffic on these bridges unless all of us are clear about the learning enterprises that are to be joined together.

WHERE SHOULD ARTICULATION EFFORTS BE CONCENTRATED?

Pre-Foreign Study

In trying to improve articulation, it is obvious that we concentrate on post-foreign studies activities, but in trying to expand the web of interconnections we should not neglect the potential in pre-foreign study course work. Accordingly, we have concentrated on two programs that can help us draw the articulation web tighter: Earlham's peace and global studies (PAGS) series and humanities program.

Earlham's PAGS series is made up of PAGS I "Culture and Conflict" (anthropology); PAGS II "The Politics of Global Issues" (political science); PAGS III "Capitalism and Socialism" (economics) and PAGS IV "Food Ethics" (philosophy). As part of our SAAP efforts, we have analyzed transcripts from the 1987 and 1988 graduating classes to determine just how close a connection there is between these courses, which are usually taken in the freshman and sophomore years and foreign study, which is usually undertaken in the junior and senior years. Our research tells us that 65% of all students who go on foreign study complete at least one PAGS course before they depart for a foreign site, which makes the series one of the most important control points in our pre-foreign study articulation work.

The four courses have always been good preparation for foreign study in that each of them provides some measure of what we have called perspective training. Students learn new ways to understand and explain global forces and issues. They learn how to read the global landscape and develop new perceptual powers and perspectives in order to understand their place and chart their way in this landscape. In workshops under the rubric of SAAP and with stipends provided by Earlham College, the regular teachers of the PAGS series worked on becoming more purposeful about their courses as preparation for foreign study. There is now a renewed emphasis in these courses as the freshman and sophomore course series that develops four types of awareness and understanding that prepare students for the foreign study experience that will likely occur in their junior and senior years.

The PAGS courses anticipate foreign study by developing four types of awareness and understanding:

1. A perspective consciousness, or awareness that individuals socialized in different cultures and societies approach reality from different perspectives, together with some understanding of the problems posed by the fact that these differing perspectives exist.

2. An understanding of global dynamics, that is to say, of the interdependence of the world system, and of several attempts to construct explanatory theories which give accounts of "how the world works."

3. An awareness of human choices, that is, of the diversity of the options and models facing humankind, and of the opportunity and responsibility to contribute to making responsible choices.

4. Knowledge of substantive issues, that is, information concerning certain of the problems that our global society confronts.

The following chart, then, shows some of the themes and topics through which the courses advance each of the four types of awareness and understanding:

	Perspective Consciousness	Global Dynamics	Human Choice	Knowledge of Problems
PAGS I *Anthropology*	Emic and etic[1] viewpoints. The relativity of values.	The embedding of cultural systems in ecosystems. Idealist and materialist explanations.	The diversity of norms and socially prescribed roles.	Gender issues. Third World development.
PAGS II *Political Science*	Differing persepctives on human rights: Western, USSR, Third World.	The logic of nuclear deterrence. Rational models as explanatory.	Alternative security systems. Environmental policy options.	Military and disarmament issues. Environmental issues. Human rights.
PAGS III *Economics*	Capitalist and socialist perspectives.	Some of the principal attempts to understand global dynamics through explanatory economic theories.	The diversity of the economic systems.	Economic aspects of class, gender, and racial discrimination and conflict.
PAGS IV *Philosophy*	Value relativism and objectivity of ethics.	Irrational rationality and its reformation.	The construction of social reality as an ongoing process.	Ideological conflicts. World hunger.

Since the awareness and understanding described above can be put to practical and specific use on a study sojourn abroad, we can claim that an on-campus classroom phase (PAGS courses) prepares students for an in-the-field phase. The developmental continuum from theory to practice has always been operant in the PAGS programs, but as a result of the SAAP project, the PAGS teachers have been able to improve the connections between the two. In a sense, nearly everything in the PAGS course is in the spirit of articulation, but new classroom activities have been added or modified as a result of the project.

1. More frequent and more explicit statements about and demonstrations of the relationships between course work on campus and off-campus study.

2. More activities that juxtapose different and equally valid conceptions of global issues such as nuclear deterrence, human rights, or resource distribution.

3. More activities that focus on cognitive theory to help students better understand how other people and groups organize reality.

4. More activities that apply learning in one context to questions in another. For example, asking students to use models demonstrated in the analysis of food or population problems to explain environmental problems.

5. More activities that enable PAGS students to apply their foreign language skills in reading course-relevant foreign language materials. Examples include Spanish language ethnographic material for "Culture and Conflict" and the foreign language original of excerpts from Kant, Pascal, and Ortega y Gasset for "Food Ethics."

6. More activities that focus on the problems of cross-cultural communication.

7. More discussion group activities that encourage students to more fully apply anthropological perspectives to their own lives in order to increase understanding of who we are in relation to the others we study.

8. More activities that explore cultural relativism and enable students, perhaps, to make moral commitments amidst such relativism.

The Humanities Program

This program—three courses taken during the freshman year—is the only core requirement at the college and aims to provide a common intellectual background for all students. In "Humanities I", students read a series of books chosen from various fields—literature, history, religion, philosophy, psychology, and others—which are the basis for class discussion and for weekly essays that are discussed and criticized in small tutorial groups. In "Humanities II" the emphasis is on four major literary and historical texts. Students are asked to discover the author's central purpose and to recognize the means by which these purposes are realized. In "Humanities II" students refine further not only fundamental skills, but also their understanding of history as related but distinct ways of making sense of human experience. Literary and historical texts include Western classics as well as works by non-Western authors. Writing assignments include a long reflective essay that draws together selected readings from all the humanities courses around a central issue or idea; students must define and defend a position of their own in this essay.

As part of the SAAP, eight senior members of the humanities teaching staff participated in a two-day workshop in June 1988. In this Ford-supported workshop, the faculty discussed the ways in which learning in our humanities program parallels learning in Earlham's foreign study programs. What commonalities exist? What differences exist? If there are similarities in the learning substance, strategies and goals of the two programs, in what ways can we see the humanities program as preparation for foreign study? If knit more closely together, would they form one learning continuum that begins in the first year on campus and continues during a study sojourn abroad?

The scheme below suggests possible connections and parallels between the programs. The list was drafted by the current director of the humanities program and the local director of the SAAP in order to stimulate discussion at the workshop.

CULTURE LEARNING	HUMANITIES LEARNING
To learn about other cultures is to explore other epistemologies, other ways of knowing and of organizing experience.	To read well is to explore other cultures, other epistemologies.
To learn about other cultures is to learn about perceptual processes and one's own place in a cultural/perceptual system.	Reading requires cultivating the imagination so that one can explore other cultures from within. Reading also requires an honest awareness of one's own cultural context and ethnocentricity.
Culture learning is immersion, living with members of another culture who impart their way of seeing and doing things.	

The goal of culture learning is to develop intercultural sensitivity, which is an increased capacity to understand, analyze, cope with, and even enjoy intercultural interaction (1.e. differentness).

The goal of reading is the conquest of provinciality, overcoming the limitations of one's place and time. Good reading is liberating.

Learners do not make progress along this continuum as the result of a series of brilliant classroom lectures. Instead, learners impel themselves along the arc of increasing sensitivity as a result of several kinds of learning: lectures, readings, classroom discussions, directed and undirected experience and, above all, reflections.

One does not become a better reader overnight; improvement comes in tiny increments through encounters with many books.

Culture learning is liberation, movement away from a limited monocultural way of seeing things toward a more flexible and varied sense of human roles and possibilities. It culminates in the capacity to begin to imagine what things might look like from the viewpoint of an insider from another culture.

Culture learning is value centered: as learners sort their way through experiences of uncertainty and relativism, they hopefully come to "apprehend the necessity of orienting themselves in a relativistic world through some form of personal commitment." (William Perry). Students are encouraged to complement their appreciation for diversity with knowledge that they can have a "home" that they can construct and defend.

A "responsible response" to a text is a reassessment of one's own values in the light of the values encountered in the text.

We have contemplated the reasons for this success in beginning such discussions with the PAGS and humanities programs. Surely the fact that we had described in detail the off-campus teaching and learning process made it easier for the on-campus faculty to imagine the ways its own work might fit into a new scheme. Perhaps, also, these faculty members are eager and productive discussants because they steward multidisciplinary programs that required from their inception a high degree of attention to collective learning outcomes and the interrelatedness among the component pieces and the participating faculty. Faculty members in such multidisciplinary programs do not merely tend to their own teaching but also must be attentive to what other faculty members are doing. It is this spirit of collective control and accountability that makes such teachers good articulators in general and makes them and their programs good points of leverage when we imagine ways to connect off-campus and on-campus learning.

Post-Foreign Study

It has been argued that sojourners return with new knowledge, skills, and sensitivity. In deciding where to concentrate our post-foreign study articulation efforts, we needed to know in what sorts of courses would there be high concentrations of returnees. The SAAP curricular effort thus required some SAAP-related research about the kinds of curricular choices returnees make. In order to maximize our articulation impact we, in theory, would have to track returnees through the remainder of their undergraduate career. Because such transcript research is unmanageable, we simply identified the academic disciplines (i.e. student majors) most frequently represented in the returnee population: 36% of all natural science majors studied abroad; 54% of all humanities majors; 59% of all social science majors. Because of the high number of social science students among the returnees, we decided to concentrate our post-foreign study articulation efforts in the social science division. The examples of our social science faculty in developing course designs and teaching strategies appropriate to improved articulation will hopefully become a model for our humanities and natural science faculties.

We have not surrendered to the difficulty of tracking our study abroad returnees in the curriculum. All participating faculty members are urged to survey their own classes to find out how many of their students studied abroad, where, and for how long. This accumulating data will help us chart future articulation work.

HOW TO ORGANIZE POST-FOREIGN STUDY ACTIVITIES

Course Surveys

If a faculty member is planning to address the need for improved articulation, it is essential to survey the students at the beginning of the term to determine who has already lived or studied abroad and who plans to do so in the near future. Only on the basis of such information will a faculty member be able to design meaningful articulation activities.

The Course Syllabus

If possible, the course syllabus should clearly state the ways returnees will have the chance to apply the knowledge, skills, and sensitivity they began to develop abroad. We do not realize the full potential of the enterprise if a special articulation activity is suddenly announced for the returnees in the fifth week of the course as an add-on assignment.

Reference in the syllabus to off-campus learning has concrete benefits. All students in the course should know that the faculty member is interested in and appreciates what is learned off-campus and that returnees will have the opportunity to apply what they have learned or the chance to further explore a topic they encountered while studying abroad. Returnees will be encouraged and future program participants will begin to see their own upcoming foreign study experience as part of a longer learning continuum and not merely a three, six, or nine month experience at a distant site. The non-foreign study population will gain a new perspective on the value of study abroad in the undergraduate curriculum.

It should be made clear that foreign study returnees will not be favored in the class. Returnees do not receive extra credit, but they do get the acknowledgment that their foreign study experience was unique, valuable, and purposeful. We would hope that in the campus culture it becomes increasingly clear that the institution values and encourages foreign study and that every formal mention of foreign study in a course syllabus or elsewhere helps program designers and operators make the point.

KINDS OF ARTICULATION ACTIVITY

Opportunities to Apply Foreign Language Skills

Many students return from foreign study with greatly improved foreign language skills and considerable interest in applying these skills. Back on the home campus, however, many of these students are frustrated to discover that except for advanced courses in literature and culture in the foreign language department, there are no curricular opportunities for them to apply their foreign language skills. Since 1980 we have been addressing this problem with our Foreign Languages in the Curriculum Program. In the period 1980 to 1984, we used grant support from the National Endowment for the Humanities to develop foreign language opportunities in courses outside the Foreign Language Department in nearly every academic discipline. This federally funded project has evolved into a successful and regular program at the college and is very much in the spirit of the SAAP—bridging the gap between off-campus and on-campus learning.

In the early years of the languages in the curriculum program, our primary interest was to make foreign language study relevant and purposeful for all of our students. Period. We still serve that original principle but have added new momentum by raising the SAAP banner. The current campus discussions about articulation can thus profitably build on an existing praxis and a supportive faculty position toward knowing and using foreign languages.

For students who return to campus eager to apply their foreign language skills as well as for students in the general campus population with at least intermediate language skills, we have evolved several general levels and types of foreign language activities outside the foreign language department. These include:

Level 1. This level does not presume advanced language skills among the students and can even be relevant to the non-foreign language speakers in the class. Faculty members introduce course-relevant terminology in the target language to demonstrate how translations fail to render the full range of connotation in the foreign language original (for example, Bildungsroman, roman à clef, or das ding an sich). It is assumed that the faculty member will then regularly refer to the original phrasing of such concepts in subsequent class lectures. Following the teacher's examples, students soon begin to use the foreign language concept in their own comments, tests, and papers.

In addition to the introduction of key concepts, a faculty member can focus on interpretive decisions required of translators of, for example, a French language original. Such discussion can address questions of content and form and become a significant linguistic as well as epistemological exercise for the students.

Level 2. For a Spanish text, read in translation by the entire class, a faculty member might ask students of the language to read a portion of the text in the original. The teacher could meet with the foreign language speakers separately and discuss in English or in Spanish select dimensions of the text of the original text. In many instances, we can prepare glossaries for text excerpts to make them accessible to students with less than perfect language skills.

Another Level 2 activity might be a history course on the Weimar Republic, for example, in which learners of German meet with the teacher to examine such materials as diplomatic dispatches or excerpts from Mein Kampf, which are not being read by the whole class. Glossaries may or may not be available.

Many of the activities at this level could also be conducted as unsupervised individual assignments. Or if a course includes formally organized discussion groups, a faculty member could designate particular sections in French, German or Spanish. On the basis of the language skills survey, faculty can assign French, German, or Spanish speakers to the appropriate group in which any of the Level 2 activities might be applied.

Level 3. High level skills and motivation are required of students who can read large amounts of foreign language materials without the help of glossaries. Students could read complete primary texts needed for their courses or could consult foreign language sources in their research assignments. Faculty members are urged to consider carefully the amount of material they expect students to read at this level. We continuously remind faculty that a single page or even a paragraph read and understood in terms of the author's original style and voice is very much a success in the spirit of this program. To have students read whole monographs or books is a worthy goal but attainable by few students.

As stated above, this program has become a regular feature of our curriculum and although it was never designed expressly to address the needs of foreign study returnees, it is in the SAAP spirit of collapsing the gap between learning at a foreign site and learning at the home campus. The campus focus on SAAP has generated renewed as well as new interest in the program. Purposeful foreign language skill using should not be limited to the few months when the students are living the culture. It can and should be possible to create skill-using opportunities across the entire home campus.

Organizing Panels of Foreign Study Returnees

In the third term of 1988 a panel of previous foreign study participants spoke in a plenary session of the course "Conflict Resolution: Theory and Technique." This course examines the problems of conflict in social theory and social affairs and studies what can make conflict amenable to non-violent resolutions. In the fourth week of this course the focus was on the ways cultural differences can incite and prolong conflict and confound attempts at resolution. In a previous session, the students had seen and discussed a film on the Iranian hostage crisis.

We have already established that learning during a study sojourn abroad is very much "perspective training." Therefore, any course that examines cross-cultural perspectives (here in terms of cross-cultural conflict) is a rich opportunity for returnees to contemplate questions of perspective and perception.

When organizing such a panel we offer these suggestions to articulators:

1. The faculty member had already queried the class about who had studied or lived abroad, who plans to do so, and who has no intention of doing so. On the basis of the survey the faculty member chose five articulate students who had already had a foreign experience. One of the five was an international student from Great Britain who was currently immersed in her own cross-cultural experience among us in Richmond, Indiana. A sixth student who had lived in Kuwait was recruited from one of the faculty member's other classes because his experience was so untypical for U.S. sojourners abroad.

2. The returnees were briefed by the faculty member before the actual panel and were asked to focus their thoughts and presentation using a set of questions. Such a briefing is essential. Without a special charge the speakers might feel compelled to give exhaustive background information on their host culture or to use the panel as a forum for their own political agenda. Or they might focus exclusively on cultural differences and not about their experience of differentness which was the actual goal of the panel.

In class, the entire session was given over to the panel speakers. The actual session and its benefits are described below.

1. These speakers, representing Kuwait, Mexico, El Salvador, the Soviet Union, and Great Britain focused on the galvanizing effect of having experienced firsthand, for example, extremes of poverty and violence. The testimony they offered seems to have a captivating effect on the forty other class participants. We suspect that the extraordinary attentiveness to the testimonies was in part due to the fact that the speakers were just like the other students in class—well-meaning, well-off, well-educated children of white professional families—but at the same time the returnees were very different. And the testimonies were offered not by a teacher as part of a lecture or discussion. The class was interested in the phenomenon (that these returnees had been transformed) and in what caused the transformation (the collision with other perceptual/cultural systems).

2. The returnees were also asked to speak to the ways that could help one better prepare to understand and cope with

intercultural interaction. To ameliorate problems of perceptual/cultural stress the returnees offered these ways of preparation for a sojourn abroad: study the values of the host culture before the trip, study their history, study our own social problems, learn their language, and know our own culture.

This carefully organized panel presentation was flawed in only one regard. The one hour session was too short to reap all of the potential in the format.

Organizing Discussion Groups

If course content and goals lend themselves to the formation of discussion groups, it is possible to identify foreign study returnees and group them together or assign them, evenly distributed, to discussion groups. This kind of activity assumes that the faculty member had previously surveyed the class to identify the returnees, their foreign study site, and so on. Faculty members who have experimented with discussion groups under the SAAP rubric make several comments and suggestions:

1. Returnees often feel isolated from their on-campus cohort and that their stay-at-home peers are not really interested in hearing about what they learned off-campus and how they have changed in terms of attitude, awareness, perspective, and behavior. A discussion group that encourages them to share aspects of their study sojourn lessens this sense of alienation.

2. Returnees in discussion groups, however, must never be allowed to simply relate their experience in an unfocused way. That will surely alienate the stay-at-home peers in the group. Returnees in discussion groups must always be very clear about what sort of input is expected from them, for example, whether it is in terms of the knowledge and insights the returnees have gained about a particular region or country or in terms of their own experience of having explored another culture's way of seeing and doing things.

3. Returnees must never be treated as the in-class "experts" on a particular region or country. They have mastered only a fragment of all there is to know about foreign countries and cultures. To expect expert opinion from them will exceed their capacities, perhaps embarrass them in front of their peers, and demonstrate to cynical teachers "that after nine months in Japan this student still doesn't really understand the Japanese educational system." A few carefully designed questions might have coaxed from just such a student what she could really

report about Japan, namely her own experiences, shoulder to shoulder with the Japanese in Japanese university classrooms.

Too often the development of new perspectives, skills, and sensitivity that begin at the foreign site is abruptly and absolutely terminated when the students return to the home campus. Whether returnees participate in discussion subsections made up exclusively of returnees from a number of foreign sites or as the only returnee in a discussion group, they are given the chance to resume the learning that began off-campus months or even several semesters earlier. Discussion groups with carefully conceived tasks and questions are an effective way to stretch the normal parameters of foreign study learning and help returnees fit their foreign study experience in a continuum that should arc all the way across their college experience.

Encouraging Connections Between Study Abroad and On-Campus Research Assignments

Anecdotal evidence suggests to us that after returning to campus sojourners often choose topics as research assignments that reflect in some way what the students had learned off campus. There may be explicit connections: classroom learning in an off-campus course on comparative european politics might lead directly to on-campus research on the European Community, NATO, or the European Parliament. In addition to direct classroom to classroom connections, there is the possibility that other kinds of on-site experiences might stimulate the sojourner's imagination to further explore a facet of the host culture in an on-campus research assignment: having seen the Japanese landscape, the East African savannah, German museum collections, or British contemporary theater, some students may choose research topics that can be traced directly to off-campus non-classroom experiences. If these connections already exist, we would like to more purposefully encourage returnees to choose research topics that build upon and continue the learning that began at a foreign site.

We offer these suggestions to improve the foreign site-home campus research connection:

1. Faculty members should indicate in course syllabi that they encourage returnees to consider research topics related to their sojourn abroad. It may be in the sense of a continuation of the off-campus classroom learning or it may be in the sense of something the students explored or experienced on their own.

2. Students may select research themes that are indeed connected to their sojourns abroad but that exceed the capacity of the campus library collection. If a topic

requires a great deal of work with non-U.S.
bibliographies, reference materials, or primary sources,
students may be seriously handicapped in their research
in the all-too-brief space of an academic term. If local
resources are clearly inadequate, faculty members should
help student researchers avoid certain topics no matter
how closely they might be linked to an off-campus
experience.

3. The faculty member may need to be somewhat yielding if
the available and appropriate resources are in foreign
languages. Only in rare instances will student researchers
have the linguistic proficiency to process material as fast
and as thoroughly as they can in English. It might be
appropriate, for example, to reduce the total number of
sources in an annotated bibliographical assignment or
make some other adjustment in the teacher's expectations
for the assignment.

Bridge Activities

Prior to departure for foreign study students will be asked to
contact one of the Earlham faculty members under whom they
will study in one of the courses they will take in the two terms
immediately following their return from foreign study (an
Earlham academic term is ten weeks long). The student and
faculty member will then define an activity to be carried out while
the student is at the foreign study site and that will in some way
find meaningful application in the faculty member's course after
the student returns to campus from foreign study.

This bridging activity that links off-campus and on-campus
studies has the following dimensions:

1. It is a bridge activity—going to see, exploring on one's own,
experiencing directly. It is not a pre-course preparatory
reading program. In fact it should in no way be seen as a
chance to force the students into an early start on
upcoming course material. It is instead an invitation for
the student to investigate and reflect upon some discrete
physical or cultural aspect of the foreign locale in terms of
what will be covered in a selected course in the student's
on-campus curriculum.

2. The bridge activity will not be a typical academic
classroom task. Supplemental reading, extensive data
gathering, researching, and reporting will not be the
modus operandi. Instead, the best bridge activities will be
those in which the faculty member provides suggestions,
signposts, and road maps to guide the students in

examining and reflecting upon some aspect of the culture or environment that otherwise might remain undiscovered by the students.

3. The bridge activity must be modest in scope and not conflict with the other formal expectations of the program on the students. We fail if it is perceived by the students as yet one more task to carry out rather than as a chance to gain new insights and make new connections that will lead to enhanced learning when the students return to campus.

4. If a student changes his or her schedule after returning from foreign study and the designated bridge course is dropped, the student will not be compelled to report to the teacher about the change in plans. Even if the in-the-field activity never finds its full expression and application in a bridge course, we can still assume that it was a valuable learning experience per se.

5. Students should also know that as a result of their in-the-field activity they will not be placed on the spot in the bridge course—they will not be required to report back in formal verbal or written form. They may or may not be called upon to comment in class at the appropriate time. And even if the faculty member forgets about the presence of a bridge student in his or her class and fails to call attention to the activity, the correlation between the in-the-field activity and the on-campus course material will still probably have become clear in the student's mind.

6. If pre-arranged in-the-field activities are not carried out, this will not result in a lower grade in the on-campus bridge course. Similarly, productive in-the-field activities will not translate into a higher grade or extra credit in the on-campus bridge course.It is possible, though, that a bridge activity will lead to papers or projects for credit in the bridge course, but bridge activities themselves must remain separate from all grading and credit-bearing activities.

7. Bridge activities will be equally meaningful whether they are in tandem with the students' major program, general education courses, or elective courses.

Benefits of the Proposed Bridge Activities

1. Generations of returnees from foreign study have reported
    with lament about the opportunities of which they failed
    to take advantage, because as explorers they were
    inexperienced, undermotivated, or underdirected. This
    regret is often phrased in a general way but is also often
    focused specifically on their post-foreign study course
    work and the realization that they failed to exploit to the
    maximum a once-in-a-lifetime learning opportunity
    abroad. Any steps we take to render the academic
    relationship between on-campus and off-campus learning
    less haphazard and more explicit will be worth our effort.

2. A bridge activity may be the only way an individual
    student's academic skills are flexed on a program that
    does not include a focus on his or her academic
    specialities. An art student on a program in Europe with a
    language, literature, and comparative politics focus would
    appreciate the suggestion to investigate a pair of
    important romanesque churches in a Paris suburb. A
    biology student on a program in Kenya with a history
    focus would benefit from the suggestion to be attentive to
    land use patterns at all the program sites.

3. For some students a side effect of foreign study is a certain
    amount of academic and affective disorientation when
    they return to the home campus. Bridge activities would
    provide more continuities between off-campus and on-
    campus experiences and could help students regain their
    balance and momentum when they return to Earlham.

4. Earlham has never viewed foreign study as a duplicate of
    the on-campus curriculum but essentially as an extension
    and expansion of what we are able to teach at the college.
    But rather than allow this learning to be perceived by the
    students as something that simply takes place somewhere
    else, we can and should easily help the students make
    their learning experience abroad fit and enhance their
    future learning on the home campus.

5. Since we want the students to bring home more than a
    boastful "I was there" attitude to their campus course
    work, we will provide, as stated above, suggestions,
    signposts, and road maps for the bridge activities. The
    insights gained, then, should be focused and of value to the
    returnees' on-campus peers too when shared in class. The
    non-foreign study students will benefit from these insights
    and the general perceived value of a study sojourn abroad
    should rise significantly.

None of these benefits are—when taken individually—great breakthroughs in the structure, substance, and strategies of foreign study programming. But the cumulative effect of up to 150 such bridge events each academic year should have, molecule by molecule, a positive overall effect on the way we design and operate foreign study in a liberal arts context. Foreign study would become part of a much longer and more significant learning continuum. Students would begin to see it less as a three, six, or nine month stay abroad after which students return home to pick up the pieces of their academic programs. Students would be encouraged to look forward as well as retrospectively and would be encouraged to find and exploit more of the interconnecting events in their undergraduate experience.

Procedures

1. In the current foreign study application process, students are required to submit a four-year academic plan. In the future, after students have been selected for the program and orientation has begun, the International Programs Office (IPO) and the program leader will expect the students to refer back to their four-year plan and choose an appropriate course from among the six they will take in their first two on-campus terms after returning from foreign study. Students will contact faculty members by the fourth week of their pre-departure orientation and work out together an appropriate bridge activity.

   It may be that the faculty member contacted is unable or unwilling to work out such a bridge activity with the student. In such instances there should still be ample time in the pre-departure term to contact other faculty members until the right connection is made.

   We expect that in many instances program leaders would also be among the faculty with whom the student would study after returning to campus. In this case we would encourage students to develop bridge activities with their program leader/upcoming teacher because the activity would probably be easier to design, the program leader could provide guidance during the actual foreign study program, and the program leader could probably guarantee a high level of articulation in the appropriate course at the home campus.

2. The bridge activity as developed by the student and faculty member will be described on a sheet that forms part of the student's original application but that had been left blank until this time. The student will indicate the course and

the faculty member and will describe the activity. We can encourage succinct description by leaving only a brief space on the form. This description will be filed in the IPO with the student's application materials. A student's application to and eligibility for a program will be considered complete only when we have this final sheet, which will also serve as our record of the scope and success of this articulation effort.

This educational scheme has implications beyond individual teacher-student relationships. In effect, we were proposing a new curriculum-wide structure and activity, another add-on responsibility of our faculty. Because such a proposal would require discussion in plenary faculty meetings, we carefully crafted our most convincing teaching and learning arguments for the scheme. In preparation, then, a number of faculty members who were supportive of the scheme were asked to provide examples of bridge activities of their own. The faculty gave us a vote of confidence for our enterprise, which surely had to do with the number and kinds of concrete examples of the scheme we were able to give. Some of these examples follow:

For the student who may enroll in "Early Modern England" upon return. After acquainting himself or herself with maps or scale models of the City of London and the City of Westminster as they were in 1500 and 1700 (London Museum, or the Barbican Museum), students could walk along the Thames River from Tower Bridge to Westminster Bridge and back by way of the Strand and Fleet Street (and then find at least most of the sites of former gates of the City of London). The object is to see the remnants of what were two cities and to discover evidence of the City of London's former separate and independent existence.

On returning, the teacher would expect the student to be ready with a description of the City of London's physical relationship to the country, one that could lead on to some analysis of the social, political, and economic relationships and its changes from the early Tudors (1500) to the late Stuarts (1700).

For the student who may enroll in "Liberal Europe." After studying some maps, the student would visit the lesser (commuter) as well as greater railway stations and go around behind them to follow out their cutting through London en route to the countryside. The student might photograph the lines as they cut through London on their way to the suburbs, exurbs, and countryside. The student should note the life alongside these lines, the object of which is to see the impact of the railway on the development of London and on patterns of London life. It is often argued that freeways have both carved up our cities and extended their development in peculiar ways. For London, it is argued, the railways had such effects.

Upon returning, the student would extend this work with some reading on London's growth and development and on the railways' impact.

For a student who will enroll in an introductory level anthropology course after study abroad. Choose several characteristics that really strike you when you arrive in the culture (e.g. relative cleanliness of the streets) and write them down. Before leaving, take out this list and look at them with more knowledgeable eyes and reflect on the changes in how you see these aspects of the culture.

Look at the culture in ecological terms. In what ways can you see ecological conditions, constraints, and opportunities influencing the culture and society of the area, or more specifically a given village, town, or city? Among the factors one might view as influential are weather, soil, and location (natural boundaries, altitude, proximity to a body of water, etc.). What patterns have been established that relate to ecological concerns?

For a student who will enroll in an advanced anthropology course after study abroad. In a rural area, what are the patterns of land ownership, and how does this affect society? Do people own their own land or work for those who do? What are the variations and the patterns? How do these patterns relate to other aspects of culture, such as politics, ethnic relations, and religious practices in the area?

For a student who will enroll in an upper level English literature course. Choose a period in literature and consider the major English painters working at that time: eighteenth century: Gainsborough, Reynolds; romantic period: Wilson, Loutherberg, Blake, Turner, Palmer, Constable; modern: Bell, Grant, Fry, and so forth. Focus on the Tate, Victoria and Albert, and Courtauld museums.

For a student on a foreign language program who will enroll in an upper level literature course. Find out who is regarded in the host culture as the most significant poet, novelist, or playwright. Who, writing in English, is most frequently compared to that writer in the second language? What are the similarities most often noted? Who has done the best-regarded contemporary English translation of that writer (if any has been done)? With what should a reader wanting to get acquainted with that writer begin?

For a student going to any site who will enroll in "Introductory Geology" or "World Geology." Observe the location of cities, roads, and agricultural land with respect to the topography of the area and location of rivers.

For a major going to Europe and who will enroll in "Geomorphology." Take along a geology map and take note of the relation of landforms to the geology of the area. Alternatively, the student could take note of glacial deposits and erosional glacial landforms in the Alps.

For a student interested in biology, particularly ecology.

1. Humans are an ecological species too! Note how patterns of agricultural land use changes with environmental conditions, (e.g. crops used, animals raised, agricultural methods, relative importance of cultivated land vs. pasturage vs. open range, or irrigated vs. non-irrigated land). How have traditional agricultural practices changed in recent times? What are the attitudes of rural people toward conservation and toward the preservation of natural ecosystems? How does this compare with attitudes expressed by urban dwellers?

2. Before leaving, read up on the natural ecosystems that exist in the country you will be visiting. Choose one that sounds particularly interesting and spend some time in that ecosystem over a weekend or during a vacation period. Take notes on the species that are present, the adaptations they have, and the environmental conditions that exist there. Once back on campus, read the primary literature that has been published by scientists on aspects of that ecosystem.

A Two-Year Experiment

We have proposed that we evaluate this articulation scheme after two full years of operation. The IPO and the International Education Committee will examine our own files for the recorded descriptions of the proposed activities and will interview selected students and faulty members about the value of the work carried out. We will then determine the ways we can improve articulation or whether the scheme should be continued at all. At that time a full report and recommendation will be made to the faculty.

Above all we feel we will be successful only if we have provided students, program leaders, and on-campus faculty with opportunities to teach and learn in new ways and to make new kinds of connections. In many regards the strength of foreign study is its open-endedness, and we do not want to put this at hazard by providing yet more structure that we have to administer. Instead, the spirit of this enterprise is to open new windows of opportunity and to encourage exploration.

NOTE

1. Emic is the study of unique features of cultures, etic is the study of common features of cultures. From Josef A. Mestenhauser, "Concepts and Theories of Culture Learning," in *Culture, Learning, and the Disciplines.* J.A. Mestenhauser, G. Marty, & Inge Steglitz (Eds.). Washington, DC: National Association for Foreign Student Affairs, 1988, p. 135.

3

KALAMAZOO COLLEGE:
STUDY ABROAD AND
FOREIGN LANGUAGE LEARNING

Joe K. Fugate

Foreign language learning, perhaps more than any other one single factor, is the key ingredient of the study abroad experience for all students except those studying in Anglophone countries. Language proficiency level frequently quite rightly decides whether or not a student will be admitted into a given program or a foreign university in the first place. More importantly, though, language proficiency determines the type of academic and personal experience the individual student will have while abroad. Whether or not the student participates actively in the foreign education system, the degree to which he or she can be integrated into daily life in the host country, have access to the media and cultural events, communicate reasonably comfortably and easily with fellow students in the classroom or dormitory, with a host family, professors, or chance acquaintances made through the activities of daily life, all are dependent on his or her ability in a foreign language. Indeed, one can safely observe that a student abroad will never feel comfortable or come to an understanding of the culture in the host country, one of the goals universally recognized for sending the student abroad in the first place, without knowledge of the host country's language.

I. STUDY ABROAD PREPARATION

If one thumbs through any of the several works on study abroad programs usually consulted by students and foreign study directors alike, one will read again and again, under the heading of eligibility, statements like two years or four semesters of college-level, or the equivalent, of Spanish, or French, or German, or whatever is required. The reason why American institutions of higher learning have generally settled on the magic number of two years or four semesters is of course directly related to the inadequate or non-existent foreign language preparation that the majority of undergraduates have experienced at the time of their enrollment at a college or university. As the recently published American Council on Education report no. 76 of September 1988 points out, 84% of the nation's four-year institutions did not have a foreign language entrance requirement in 1986. For those that did, two years of high school training was the accepted norm, which, as any foreign language teacher knows, is hardly enough to be of any consequence. Since most institutions continue to send their students abroad in the junior year, colleges and universities have only two years or four semesters in which to prepare the student linguistically. By comparison, students in other education systems, including those in developing countries, often arrive at the university with five to seven years of language study in one or more foreign languages. At best this will mean that American students studying abroad are linguistically disadvantaged when compared with students from other educational systems. I was reminded dramatically of this when I recently visited an English to French translation class in a French university. While designed for Anglophones, a number of the participants did not speak English as their native language. It was clear, however, that their proficiency in English was sufficient to enable them to more than hold their own with the native Anglophones. This state of affairs is likely to have increasingly serious ramifications for American students studying in Western Europe as student mobility increases there through the implementation of ERASMUS (Expanded Regional Action Scheme for the Mobility of University Students).

No one could disagree with the judgment that two years is insufficient to prepare a student adequately for serious study in another language. The fact that many of our students have successful experiences abroad with only these two years of prior preparation speaks well for the training that they receive, inadequate though it may be. Nevertheless, the question constantly facing foreign language professors and directors of study abroad programs is how best to utilize the time available in order to bring the students to the highest level of proficiency possible. As is the case with most matters in American higher education, there are endless variations and opinions in this area, but there do seem to be several patterns that can be identified and isolated.

1. Since the percentage of undergraduates studying abroad in most institutions remains relatively small, no attempt is made to separate those who will study abroad from the student who is studying a foreign language to meet the language requirement or for any other reason. As far as I can tell from speaking with colleagues, this seems to be the norm.

2. In a few institutions an effort is made to do a special course for those who plan to study abroad. In some cases this takes the form of an intensive course in the last semester preceding study abroad.

3. For some of the less commonly taught languages there is the requirement of an intensive summer course prior to departure. While some of these courses are for students with prior training, others will represent the only exposure to the foreign language for the American student before arriving in the host country.

Regardless of what method or combination of methods are employed on the home campus, the big question is of course how well the students will be able to function once they arrive overseas and how their competency in the language will be perceived by native speakers in general and our foreign colleagues in particular. My experience confirms three main problem areas, irrespective of language and country, that are mentioned over and over again by our colleagues abroad: (1) lack of vocabulary, (2) lack of oral proficiency, and (3) the tendency on the part of the American students to equate exposure with mastery, particularly when it comes to grammar. So there can be no misunderstandings, let me say here that I refer above to the more commonly taught Western European languages, which still attract the majority of students going abroad. The less commonly taught languages, particularly those with radically different writing systems, present the problems listed above and others too. Although the numbers of students pursuing studies in these languages while abroad is increasing, few if any undergraduates are enrolled directly in a host institution pursuing a course of study entirely in the target language.

There are very good reasons why the first two points mentioned above are recurring themes in conversations with language teachers abroad. After all, there is a limit to what can be achieved with between 200 to 250 classroom contact hours, particularly when the foreign language course will be only one of several in which students are enrolled at a given time. It is always more difficult to re-create a foreign language atmosphere on an American campus than when abroad. In the area of vocabulary, much of what immediately becomes critical for survival once one arrives in a foreign country seems far in the distant future for the student who is struggling through the second or third semester course and does not quite understand why it is necessary to know such a mundane phrase as "plug in the toaster" or how to get a pair of shoes repaired. Over the years it has been my observation that it is this lack of ability to function on a survival level that is most frustrating to the students upon their arrival overseas. What any child would know and be able to express, the university level student cannot—not always a terribly comfortable feeling!   The lack of oral proficiency is of course intimidating, and after a few experiences of not being understood often results in the student's reducing all communication in the foreign tongue with locals to a minimum and restricting social contacts to fellow Americans or others who speak English.

While keeping the above points in mind, let us take a look at what is happening and what should be happening in the language courses that prepare a student for study abroad.   The first two years of language study seem to run something like this: in the first and second semesters students work through a basic grammar book and are at least exposed to the basic principles of the foreign language, acquire a minimal vocabulary, and, if they are lucky, are given some aural-oral training in the language.   In the second year there is further grammar review and more readings.   In some cases there is an opportunity to enroll in a conversation class or a composition course.   The number of contact hours in the foreign language will probably not amount to more than 250 under the most optimal circumstances.   All instruction, except beginning grammar explanations, would ideally be in the target language, and students would be required to respond in the target language.   The language professor will also hopefully be continuously mindful of the cultural context of the language taught.   If language laboratory facilities are available, these facilities should be used to the maximum to enrich the basic classroom instruction.   And finally, the instructor should be aware of what will be expected of students once they arrive overseas.   Whereas twenty or twenty-five years ago it was perhaps an unreasonable demand to place on many instructors, in this day and age there can be no excuse for an effective language teacher not to have spent some time abroad.

A variety of activities and arrangements outside of the classroom can be instituted to aid the students in acquiring practical experience in using the target language and in overcoming their reluctance to communicate in it.   Language houses, where the target language is the sole medium of communication, language tables, interactions with students from abroad, films, videotapes, and so on—the whole panoply of devices known to any experienced language teacher—have been tried and tested and found successful in helping to motivate and stimulate the students in their efforts to raise their level of competency.

No one method or combination thereof can guarantee success. Rather, if the goal of maximum active facility in the language within the limits imposed by the time restrictions is attained, then the preparation can most certainly be seen as successful by students and faculty alike.

If a program or institution has made a decision to begin the language study abroad, then most, if not all of the above discussion will be inapplicable.   Personally, I find myself in the camp of those who would argue against this approach since I believe that the student who arrives without some knowledge of the language of the host country, be it ever so rudimentary, sacrifices too much time and effort in acquiring the minimal knowledge necessary to function on even the most elementary level in the culture. I would agree with those who see this as counter productive to the goals most commonly set for study abroad in the first place.

II. CONTINUED REFINEMENT WHILE ABROAD

Three basic patterns stand out among the endless variation of systems employed once the student arrives abroad: (1) Beginning students with little or no prior knowledge of the language are taught as a group by their accompanying American professors or by locally appointed professionals. In some cases students are attached individually or by groups to established foreign language teaching centers or institutes, such as the Goethe Institut or the Alliance Française, to name only two. The third variation of this basic pattern is to place the beginning student in language courses for foreign students at academic institutions. (2) American students with prior language training are sent abroad as a group and are instructed by the accompanying American faculty member. Local instructors are also used, but they are closely supervised by the accompanying American faculty member or members. (3) American students who have a basic knowledge of the language, usually measured in terms of courses not proficiency, are expected to integrate as fully as possible into the educational system of the host country. This means that all continued language instruction will be by professionals who are teaching their own native tongue as a second language.

The one issue that is guaranteed to surface yearly in any study abroad program with a foreign language component is the appropriateness of the language teaching. Foreign study directors' reports regularly fill pages commenting on the reception of language instruction by the students and on the instructors' reaction to the students' prior preparation and continued improvement while abroad. The lack of agreement one often finds among American instructors as to what methods are best utilized at home or abroad are intensified by the responses and judgments of foreign colleagues. American foreign language teachers are often critical of what happens to their students once they are abroad, while those teaching abroad are sometimes disdainful of the methods and results of their American counterparts. Add to this the American student's reaction to the new and different systems of teaching, and the result is that foreign language teaching of American students abroad presents an ongoing problem that never seems to be completely resolved to the total satisfaction of all parties concerned.

The easiest and least troublesome option is to have the American student instructed by American faculty. Whether this choice will produce the most effective results or whether it is compatible with the goals of exposing a student to another culture in another educational system is of course a different matter. Concerning these two issues there are serious disagreements, but more on that later. In those cases in which professors from the home campus instruct the students, more often than not there is a transferral of what happens on the home campus to the foreign location with the added attraction of being able to use the local surroundings as a living laboratory. The student is spared the necessity of adjusting to different pedagogical methods and expectations but will hopefully be motivated and stimulated by being in an atmosphere where the language studied is in constant use. Under these circumstances the skillful American language instructor who understands how to exploit to the fullest the advantages of teaching American students a foreign language in situ can justifiably be pleased with the remarkable progress that students often make in a relatively short period of time.

However, if my observations are correct, the majority of American students pursuing foreign language study abroad are not taught by American instructors. This of course means that the control that a foreign language department exercises over methods and content when the instruction is by a member of that department is now partially or totally lost. While instructors at foreign institutions will often be receptive to suggestions from American colleagues, for the most part the content and the methods used in the courses will be determined locally, and not by the American institution. This is true even for courses commissioned specifically for American students, as after all the instructors are generally the products of their own educational system and reflect its philosophy and methods. If in international education we believe what we say about wanting to immerse our students in another culture and its institutions, then having American students taught foreign languages by native speakers of that language in the country where the language is spoken should be an integral part of any foreign study program. As anyone in international education knows, this does create problems. Why?

American students are often openly critical of the language instruction they receive in foreign institutions. Is this criticism justified? The answer is a mixed one. To state the obvious, there is instruction of excellent quality abroad and there is instruction of poor quality abroad, just as we have at home. My observation over a period of twenty-five years is that the basic problem lies not with the quality of the instruction, but rather in the fact that it is different. The philosophy, the goals, and the methods, not to mention the instructor's classroom manner, represent a profound change for American students from that to which they are accustomed. That American students are notoriously critical of other educational systems and resist adapting to them has been well established by major research.

Several examples in the area of foreign language instruction will serve to illustrate the problem. In the United States a typical study plan in a foreign language course will call for our covering of a certain amount of material in a given time. That material will be presented by the instructor, with varying degrees of mastery of the material on the part of the student. Generally though, the instructor will cover the material as planned and the marks of the students will reflect the degree to which they have mastered the material. When the American student transfers this way of thinking to the language instruction class abroad, he or she has difficulty coming to terms with a class in which the instructor requires a demonstrated grasp of a point before continuing. I have lost count of how many times students have complained to me that an instructor was reviewing some point or the other that they had already had, notice the word "had," in the second or third level course. The problem was, of course, that they might have been exposed to it, but as their performance clearly illustrated, they had failed to master it.

Second, American students are accustomed to courses in which the instructor is expected to be entertaining, interesting, and stimulating. Students expect that explanations will be given in English, with the material laid out in such a way that they have to make little effort to find answers to their questions. In other countries they suddenly find themselves in a system where the teacher is a guide and helper but certainly not usually a stimulator or one who is going to do the work for the student. Foreign colleagues frequently observe that the American students fail to understand that they must master the material and that this cannot be done for them by the teacher.

American students often arrive abroad with the expectation that texts and classroom explanations will be in English, just like they were at home. I was forcefully reminded of this while preparing this paper when I was visited by one of our students who unexpectedly returned home for a few days for family reasons and who called upon me to report on how things were going. When I questioned her about the language classes, she replied that she and the others were disappointed on two counts: the students didn't like the text they were using that had been produced by the foreign university, and they were also unhappy because their language teacher did not speak English and did not give grammar explanations in English. She was somewhat shocked when I questioned the students' perceptions and explained why I thought that it was perfectly normal for the teacher to instruct in the target language.

Recently a colleague and I had a discussion with a group of students who were unhappy with the communicative techniques that a language instructor abroad was using with them. Both of us were very pleased with the instruction, while it was apparent that at least some in the class had been unable to see the sense behind the teacher's method because it was new and different.

While it is highly unlikely that it will ever be possible to resolve some of these problems once and for all, there are ways to bring the divergent points of view closer together. First and foremost, there is the responsibility of a foreign study program to prepare the student for the experience abroad, and this includes an orientation concerning the educational system and methods that the student will encounter while abroad. If there is a resident U.S. director or if there are visits by people from the home campus, these points need to be reinforced and put into perspective after the students have become actual participants in the foreign system. Second, the students need to be reminded as forcefully as possible that they are the ones, and not the foreign system, who will have to adapt and change. In my estimation, this is perhaps the single most important prerequisite for success on the part of the student, for an appropriate mind-set and a positive attitude will make the student receptive to the offerings of the foreign system. Communication between colleagues at home and abroad and an exchange of materials and information are all useful and important but hardly to the same degree as having students prepared and sufficiently flexible to adapt to and accept the givens of a different system.

Foreign language acquisition has been traditionally established as one of the main reasons for sending a student abroad. For the American this goal is certainly as urgent today as at any time in our history. It thus behooves every American study abroad program with a foreign language dimension and all those associated with the program to establish a structure that will facilitate the attainment of maximum proficiency in the foreign language. Anything less than this is to question the basic raison d'être of such a venture in the first place. Those of us involved with study abroad know that it is not the instruction alone that produces these results, but the instruction does without a doubt provide the launching pad and the foundation for attainment of the ultimate goal of foreign language mastery. All available evidence supports the conclusion that those students who have studied abroad achieve by far and away the highest level of proficiency in foreign languages of any students in our educational system.

III. MAINTENANCE OF FOREIGN LANGUAGE SKILLS AFTER THE RETURN HOME

How to integrate of study abroad with the on-campus program is one of the perennial questions confronted by those engaged in international education. Students returning from abroad often find it impossible to continue on the home campus in areas in which they have developed interests while abroad. In addition, it seems that many faculty members frequently are unable to appreciate or relate to the newly acquired knowledge and experience of the returnees. Students who have worked hard and acquired a reasonable degree of fluency in a foreign language are often unable to pursue further formal study of the language upon their return home because of scheduling problems or major course requirements. In particular, the complaint is often heard from students that they have few, if any, opportunities to apply their foreign language knowledge in courses outside of those taught in the foreign language departments.

For the language specialist—a major, double major, or minor—there should be few if any difficulties in this area. The curricula and courses in the overwhelming majority of American institutions are specifically designed for this group of students. It should hardly be necessary to observe that language departments and instructors have a responsibility to organize the course offerings in such a way as to take advantage of the presence of students who have had practical experience in the language and who have studied in a country in which it is spoken. At the very least the returnee should be able to assume that all courses will be taught in the target language and that those teaching the courses will have a command of the language and a knowledge of the foreign area and its culture superior to that of the returnee. A returnee is hardly likely to be challenged by or very tolerant of instructors whose language proficiency is dated or inferior to their own.

Study abroad, however, is not an experience that we wish to have restricted to the language specialist alone. Those concerned with international education in its broadest sense, and this means both on and off campus, must continue their attempts to increase the numbers of non-language or area specialists who study foreign languages and study abroad. My own institution, Kalamazoo College, with a participation in study abroad of over 85% of each graduating class for more than twenty years, is an example of one institution that has had some success in this area. Clearly the majority of our students who study abroad are not language specialists. Many of them return home excited by their experiences and motivated to continue their study of the language, only to find that there are almost no course-related opportunities available for further development of their linguistic skills except in the foreign language departments. A number of foreign language extraclassroom activities are available, but it is well known that in the majority of cases these alone will hardly suffice for the mere maintenance of the students' hard-won language skills, let alone going beyond the level of proficiency already attained while abroad.

What could or should institutions be doing to speak to the needs of this group of study abroad returnees? One strategy is to attempt to include a foreign language component in a variety of courses in the overall curriculum and not relegate the use of foreign language skills to the foreign language departments alone. Implementation possibilities here range from actually teaching and conducting a class in another language to including a list of suggested readings in another language or languages. These and several other options that lie between the two poles would all afford our students further opportunities to develop their language skills and would reinforce the logic of learning a foreign language in the first place.

Critical to any such attempt on a campus is of course the language competency of the teaching faculty and the willingness of individual members of the faculty to engage in such ventures, whether by offering to teach a course in another language, developing appropriate reading materials and encouraging students to make use of them, or even accepting papers written in another language. The appropriateness of one or the other of the above approaches is obvious in a subject matter area that has direct relevance to a foreign culture or language. Thus, for example, in a course in German history one could assume that the instructor would have some knowledge of German and would be happy to include German titles in the bibliography. In other areas, natural sciences or economics for example, the relevance of foreign language material is not so apparent, at least at first glance.

As has already been noted, the role of the faculty in the implementation of an adventure of this type is obviously a critical one. If we may regard my own institution as a norm, an institution that is generally recognized for its commitment to international studies, then the need for internationalizing the faculty, particularly in the area of foreign language competency, is perhaps even greater than that of the students. A survey of the teaching faculty at Kalamazoo College outside of the foreign language departments resulted in some interesting data. More than 31% of this group indicated no competence whatsoever in a foreign language. Not surprisingly, the natural science and economics departments had the largest concentration here. Non-native speakers, and the number here is small, were capable of lecturing or conducting a class discussion only in French, Spanish, or German. One faculty member responded that he purposely had not ordered any foreign language titles for the library, while another remarked that in science everything is in English.

The data collected from my survey, coupled with the fact that I know the entire faculty and their foreign language competence personally, permit several general conclusions:

1. The overall language competency of Kalamazoo College students is generally higher than that of the faculty.

2. While a number of faculty members have studied foreign languages and have at least some passive knowledge of one or more languages, the number who have an active command of a foreign language and who would be able to function reasonably and easily in another language is small.

3. There is a reservoir of good will and interest on the part of many on the faculty to apply language knowledge to their courses and to make it possible for students to work in a foreign language.

4. Much work would have to be done to aid faculty in upgrading or refreshing their knowledge of foreign languages if there were to be extensive use of students' foreign language knowledge in a variety of courses.

Thus a possible remedy that would provide a solution to the non-language specialist's dilemma of not being able to continue with active study of the language after returning from study abroad has, in turn, identified a further problem in the area of faculty development. In Kalamazoo's and other analogous situations several courses of action suggest themselves:

1. That those faculty who are able and willing to do so be encouraged to add foreign language dimensions to their courses wherever they fit or are possible.

2. That a formal program of faculty development in the area of languages be implemented.

3. That appropriate library resources be acquired so that students can work in a foreign language in a variety of disciplines.

4. That a campus-wide effort be made to encourage students to maintain and continue to develop foreign language competency.

Acquiring and maintaining proficiency in a foreign language is not a process that terminates after the return of the student from study abroad. Indeed, in many ways it is only the beginning. It would be tragic to admit that after an investment of much time and energy the process would be considered completed. Those of us engaged in international education certainly have the responsibility to students to ensure that a continuation of this process, by means suggested above and others, will be possible as long as they remain in the academy. By the time they leave the academy, they hopefully will have convinced themselves of the necessity and validity of maintaining and adding to their language competency by whatever means possible and regardless of their chosen occupation.

CONCLUSION

Hopefully I have been able to demonstrate that the relation between foreign language learning and study abroad involves an ongoing process that spans most, if not all, of a student's undergraduate career. The pre-departure preparation, the ongoing study of language while abroad, and the opportunity after returning to continue using the language both in and outside of the classroom each represent an important step in this process. The first two of these steps have traditionally demanded most of our time, energy, and attention. Although the achievements here are considerable, we would all agree that there is much room for additional improvement. The third step in our process, however, seems largely to have been ignored on all but a few campuses. Here the field is wide open for new and innovative strategies that will help students to maintain and improve their language competency and to continue further the process of internationalization both as individuals and members of the campus community as a whole.

4

THE UNIVERSITY OF CALIFORNIA: FACULTY SUPPORT, THE NEEDED LINK

Theda Shapiro

The University of California currently has eight campuses granting undergraduate liberal arts degrees. In the UC system the faculty has major responsibility for the curriculum and each campus has considerable autonomy over its educational programs. In 1989 and 1990, the undergraduate student enrollment of the university was approximately 124,500. The University has its own university-wide study abroad structure, the Education Abroad Program (EAP), which is currently sending some 1,500 undergraduates yearly, about 4.8 % of each student cohort, to some eighty-five locations in thirty-three countries throughout the world. Many additional students—possibly an equal number to those participating in the EAP, although recordkeeping is inexact—enroll in a myriad of external study abroad programs. On some campuses, such as San Diego and Santa Cruz, both EAP and other opportunities are strongly encouraged and assisted; on others, EAP is well supported, but students going abroad through other programs are largely on their own. At present almost all of the EAP offerings are year-long academic programs in which the students are integrated directly into foreign universities; however, one-semester and summer programs are being instituted, and while these raise new concerns about the purposes of EAP and the credibility of its academic standards, they should appeal to students in highly specialized majors who are often discouraged or impeded from studying abroad.

In one major respect the University of California is unusual among the institutions that participated in the Study Abroad Articulation Project (SAAP): it is the only one of the three large, public universities whose study abroad program represents all campuses of the system and has a large central office (located on the Santa Barbara campus) that formulates policy and coordinates local participation. Thus it has a complex administrative structure—EAP functions simultaneously on eight different campuses and in a central administrative office, as well as abroad—and the necessity of articulating the curricula of eight home campuses with those followed by the students abroad. While the student is virtually guaranteed graduation units for successfully completing academic courses on EAP, each campus has considerable responsibility for pre-departure preparation and complete autonomy in the assignment of credit toward breadth (requirements to ensure students' college education gives them some acquaintance with the humanities, social sciences, and sciences, and in some case with cultural diversity) and major requirements for work completed abroad.

The climate within the university for this sort of self-study has been very receptive. University President David P. Gardner is a warm supporter of international education who wishes for the opportunities available to UC students abroad to multiply during the coming years. The Education Abroad Program itself is experiencing a time of transition, with the recent retirement of its founder and longstanding director and new curricular and geographic emphases in its programs. The San Diego campus has recently inaugurated its new Fifth College, which requires all students to have a study abroad experience. The university is growing rapidly—in fact, too rapidly for comfort—and its enrollment is becoming more and more diversified ethnically, as it reflects the changing population of the state of California. Also, within the California State Legislature there is a growing awareness of the interdependence of countries, languages, and cultures, and of the importance of greater reciprocity between UC and foreign universities to foster the university's research mission, which directly contributes to the economic welfare of the state. Thus, the light shed by this study on the current situation and future goals of study abroad is being received with great interest.

For the purpose of manageability, an initial decision was to limit the SAAP study to three of the university's small and medium-sized campuses: Irvine, Riverside, and San Diego, all located in Southern California. It was also decided to examine only the Education Abroad Program. This latter choice was made because the EAP is the official study abroad program of the university and enrolls such a large number of students. As the "accredited" program, it is the EAP that has the obligation to provide the university with high-quality instruction wherever it has a center and that promises the student a high degree of integration of courses taken abroad with home-campus studies.

THE STUDY OF CURRICULAR ARTICULATION BETWEEN CAMPUSES AND THE EDUCATION ABROAD PROGRAM

In order to study the articulation between academic work done on EAP and the curricula of the three target home campuses, the committee examined the transcripts and related material concerning 580 students who had participated in the program between 1980 and 1981 and 1985 and 1986. All undergraduates participating in EAP are juniors or seniors; they are required to have a pre-departure grade point average of 3.0 (B) or higher, although 15% of those in the sample were permitted to enroll in the program with slightly lower grades. The committee interpreted the concept of articulation broadly, embracing problems of pre-departure selection and preparation as well as eventual curricular outcomes. The most salient discoveries and conclusions follow:

Demographic characteristics of EAP students. Not surprisingly, the students in the sample are predominantly female (67.5%) and Caucasian (78.2%). Among the large minority groups, only Hispanics have participated in EAP in anything like equitable numbers (14.4%). Both findings, on gender and ethnicity, seem partially to stem from students' choices of major and from the different affinities of various disciplines for study abroad (see below). On the home campuses women students are preponderant in the humanities and social sciences, by a margin of approximately 60% to 40%, but they are even more so in the EAP. The low number of black, Asian, and other minorities in EAP seems to be related to economic and cultural factors, such as the financial burden of both the cost of study abroad and lost income at home, and a relatively low level of interest in foreign places or languages, as well as academic factors such as choice of major or level of grade point average.

We concluded that new types of EAP opportunities, heightened faculty awareness, and improved counseling will be necessary to attract students in the low-participation groups, be they male students, minorities, or students in the sciences and professional schools. In particular, the complex problems of minorities in relation to study abroad merit close examination. What measures might make language learning and foreign study more attractive to these students or might ease the financial burdens?

An additional demographic finding of the study is the large presence of seniors, who made up about one-third of the EAP students in the sample. We found that little special attention is given these students pre-departure, even though many of them intend to graduate directly upon completion of EAP. In fact, many are forced to return to their home campuses for additional course work, or find their graduation delayed because grades are slow to arrive from abroad. In their case, counseling should be more diligent and thorough than it is now.

Retention. In the sample, the withdrawal rate from the EAP was zero, although a few students completed only a partial program. At least 90% of the participants later graduated from their home campuses. Retention of these students, therefore, was found to be excellent, both within the EAP and at the home campuses.

Relations between academic disciplines and study abroad. Unsurprisingly, there is considerable disproportion between the campus enrollments in various majors and the mix of study abroad students. In our sample, about 40% of the EAP students were in the humanities, 30% in social science, and only 20% in science, among whom half were studying biological sciences. (The remaining 10% were either undeclared or in professional programs.) This disproportion raises serious questions about the lack of exposure to international experience of students who will eventually have professional careers in the sciences, medicine, business, and technical fields. New sorts of programs, more integrally related to the scientific and technical disciplines, will be needed to attract and serve these students. While the assessment of the structural conditions necessary for realistic improvement in this area will take time, academic advising might more rapidly be improved, so as to make possible better integration of courses available abroad with both breadth and major requirements.

Changes of major. Of the 563 students in our sample who had declared a major prior to departure, only 15% changed to another major before graduation. As a result of both first declarations and changes of major, the humanities gained a net five students, the social sciences gained eleven, and the sciences lost six—no substantial "brain drain" toward the humanities, as is often assumed.

On the other hand, 18% of the students had a double major by the time of graduation, and many dropped, changed, or acquired second majors during or as a direct result of study abroad. Here the humanities—and not just the language/literature programs—enrolled quite a few students, the social sciences a moderate number, and the sciences only a few, as students found their academic work taken abroad conducive to the acquisition of a second major.

Course load. At this time, almost all EAP offerings abroad are year-long programs that require full-time participation with the completion of a minimum of 36 quarter units (the equivalent of nine UC courses). On average, the students in the sample completed 44.5 quarter units abroad, a load that makes it very nearly possible to complete the 180 units required for graduation in exactly four years. About 10% of the students earned fewer than the required full-time load; this probably compares quite favorably with the numbers of less-than-full-timers on the home campuses.

Students participating in the EAP did seem to take a few more courses before graduation than home campus students. The EAP students, on average, had 208 units at graduation, and the science students among them averaged about 220 units. While the frequent acquisition of second majors may explain some of the excess, clearly study abroad made possible—or necessary—the taking of additional elective courses or the enrichment of majors.

Time to graduation. The average time from freshman entry to graduation for our EAP participants was 13.3 quarters (about 4.4 years), only slightly in excess of current home campus averages. Over 47% of the study abroad students graduated in four years or less, although another 37% took 4.5 to 5 years. Contrary to faculty opinion, the committee concluded that EAP participation did not excessively delay students' graduation.

Credit for work completed while abroad. Here, of course, is the major practical question of articulation: how is the academic work completed by the student abroad applied to the curricular requirements on the home campus?

As was mentioned above, one way in which EAP differs from many other study abroad programs is that it virtually guarantees unit credit on the home campuses for work completed through one of its centers abroad. This is achieved by the transformation, on paper, of all courses taken abroad into UC-equivalent courses, which are then examined, revised if necessary, and approved by the appropriate faculty committees on the Santa Barbara campus. In our examination of student transcripts we found that this system works well: in only very few cases was unit credit toward graduation denied—the mean difference between units taken and units credited being only .03 units. It seems that the occasional denial of units stems from a lack of an equivalent subject matter on a home campus or scepticism about the academic value of a given course, but it is so infrequent as to cause no alarm. None of the three target campuses had any stated limit as to the number of units it would accept from EAP. In fact, 108 students in the sample had transferred 51 or more units for work completed abroad.

When we looked at credit given toward breadth and major requirements, however, we found serious problems. In particular, students typically receive little or no credit toward breadth requirements. On average, each participant in the sample received credit for only one course; in fact, 72% of the students received no credit at all toward breadth requirements, and the others were usually credited with two or more courses. Since all EAP participants are upperclassmen, they might have completed all their breadth courses before departure, although students in general do not typically do so during their first two years. We questioned whether pre-departure academic counseling might be strengthened, so as to help the student make the greatest possible academic use of the courses available abroad. In particular, students who can anticipate that they will not be able to complete substantial major requirements abroad should be counseled to plan on completing breadth requirements instead.

The credit given toward major requirements presented a generally better, but much more varied, picture. On average, the students in the sample received credit for about five courses in their major for work completed abroad, but there was considerable variation by discipline. Students received credit for about six courses in the humanities, four to five in the social sciences, five to six in the biological sciences, four in the physical sciences, and three in the mathematical sciences and business/administration. While these numbers are generous compared to the credit granted toward breadth requirements, we also noted that 22.4% of the students in the sample received no credit at all toward their major requirements. The others completed 20% to 50% of their major requirements while abroad.

Evolution of EAP participants' grades. The examination of the grade point averages of the students in the sample before, during, and after their study abroad experience was astonishing: we found them practically flat. On average, the grades went up slightly during EAP but came down again nearly to their previous levels at graduation. We found this no cause for alarm, since these students were well above average before, during, and after EAP, with mean GPAs in the B+ range. But it seems curious, nevertheless, that the rigors of adaptation to a new culture and educational system, most often including functioning academically in a foreign language, did not show up, after an initial period of "reverse culture shock," in overall improvement of grades on the home campus.

As mentioned above, 15% of the students in the sample had been admitted to the program with slightly less than the required GPA of 3.0. All these students completed their study abroad programs in good standing, and some of them had improved GPAs by graduation.

Participants' reinsertion into their home campuses. Our study was ill equipped to provide clarification about student returnees' reintegration into the academic and cultural life of their home campuses, but we know, based on annual questionnaires completed by returning EAP students and from anecdotal evidence gathered at on-campus EAP offices, that returning students feel alienated on the home campuses. Virtually no efforts are currently made to either help the students academically digest the knowledge and experiences gained abroad or to apply their experience to enrich on-campus life. The benefits of study abroad seem to accrue entirely to the individual student in relative isolation from home campus education, whereas they might be shared with others and also might result in further intellectual enrichment for the student were they applied to course work, seminars, or honors theses.

In conclusion, the committee found that the Education Abroad Program does an excellent job for the students in many areas: it attracts highly qualified students, retains them, maintains their full-time activity within the university, and returns them to their home campuses in academic standing comparable to when they left. But we found some serious deficiencies in articulation. The EAP is not enrolling male students, science and professional majors, and most ethnic minorities in equitable numbers. These students, and also those who participate as seniors, are not receiving sufficiently skilled counseling so as to make study abroad feasible and to capitalize on the available opportunities. Students are not awarded adequate credit toward breadth requirements and, in many departments, toward major requirements, for courses taken abroad. Little attention is paid to the students' reinsertion into the life of their home campus, to the ways in which their education might be enriched after study abroad, or to the ways in which they might contribute to internationalizing
on-campus instruction.

THE SURVEY OF FACULTY OPINION

In order to assess the attitudes of faculty members toward study abroad in the University of California context, the committee distributed a questionnaire to all faculty members on the three target campuses. We obtained a total of 586 replies, representing a fairly good cross-sectional response both across the three campuses and across disciplines, and including about 25% of the permanent faculty on each campus.

The questionnaire asked about faculty members' experience with the EAP and with EAP students, their assessments of the academic quality of EAP students, their opinions as to the major benefits and drawbacks of participation in EAP, and their general levels of support for study abroad in general and the EAP in particular. The responses were examined for each campus and in the aggregate, by the respondents' academic disciplines, and by the respondents' own travel experience. The major findings are as follows.

Faculty experience with the EAP program and its students. We found that the majority of the faculty polled considered themselves ignorant about the Education Abroad Program, and only 56% said they were acquainted with EAP students. The results were yet more striking when examined according to academic disciplinary groups: in the language-related departments, only 24% of the respondents had no experience with EAP and all respondents knew EAP students, whereas 61% of social scientists, 72% of those in biological science, and 82% of those in business/administration had no experience with EAP, and 37% of social scientists, 43% of physical scientists, and 73%

of faculty members in business/administration knew no EAP students. Foreign born faculty members or those who had lengthy experiences abroad were much more likely to be acquainted with the EAP and its students than those with little travel or foreign language experience. It seemed obvious to us that the current methods of informing or involving faculty do not adequately reach faculty who are not already oriented toward study abroad through their own academic specializations or travel experiences.

Faculty assessment of academic quality of EAP students. About 95% of the respondents considered EAP students to be somewhat or much better academically than the average student. There was little variation in the responses according to the respondent's academic discipline or travel experience. Those faculty who considered themselves ignorant about EAP tended to skip this question.

Benefits of participation in the EAP. When asked about possible benefits of study abroad, the highest affirmatives came in the rather broad category "personal growth," and many added "cultural awareness," "tolerance," and "maturity," all categories we might call "experiential" rather than intellectual. On the more specifically academic benefits there was greater divergence of opinion. Not surprisingly, a majority of humanities faculty members saw EAP as directly relevant to the major, while only a minority of other faculty members did. A large majority of all respondents felt that study abroad fosters the students' academic development in general, but humanities and social science faculty members were more convinced than others that it improves career or further educational opportunities.

We concluded that while almost all faculty members feel that study abroad is beneficial in terms of general maturity and intellectual growth, there is no consensus as to what study abroad should accomplish within the academic framework of a college education. The development of a greater sense of academic relevancy would certainly make the "non-study-abroad disciplines" more receptive to increased participation of their students. Here, only the faculty can assume leadership in developing more receptive attitudes and in creating more relevant programs for the under represented areas.

Drawbacks of participation in the EAP. Faculty members were also asked to respond to a series of suggested drawbacks of EAP participation. A few felt that study abroad lowers the academic quality of the students' education (12%), disrupts their personal lives (6%), impedes their professional development (7%), or unduly depletes departmental enrollments (8%). A more substantial number felt that it considerably interrupts progress toward the degree (24%) or delays graduation (21%). On these last two points, the responses from outside the humanities and the social sciences were often negative. Twenty-seven percent of faculty members in the biological sciences, more than 33% in the physical sciences,

42% in the mathematical sciences, and 45% in business/administration felt that EAP interrupts progress toward the degree; while 29% in the physical sciences, 37% in the mathematical sciences, and 30% in business/administration felt it substantially delays graduation.

We have shown above that in actual fact, while EAP participation may interrupt progress in the major for those in the scientific and professional fields, it only slightly delays graduation for most students. Those faculty members who do not see the direct academic relevance of EAP to their areas of specialization are more prone than others to harbor doubts about the contributions of study abroad to their students' curriculum and about its disruptive effects on their students' lives.

General faculty support for study abroad. Faculty members were asked to express their general levels of support, high or low, for international education and more specifically for the Education Abroad Program. Here the response was very affirmative: only 9% of the respondents expressed a low level of support for study abroad and 13% for the EAP. In every disciplinary group a large majority, ranging from about 70% to 100%, gave one of the high responses to both questions. The degree of enthusiasm in the positive responses seemed to be correlated to the respondents' own levels of international experience. Clearly, faculty members expressed high support for study abroad even if they differed in their understanding of its specific outcomes.

RECOMMENDATIONS

The Education Abroad Program has done a fine job of educating students abroad for the last twenty-eight years, and our study found much to praise in its current operations. But EAP must also adapt to accommodate new student publics and to cooperate more fully in the internationalized perspectives of science, communications, technology, and business with which we now live. Because of the strong role of the university's faculty in curricular development, the key to such a transformation within the University lies with them, not primarily with EAP's administration. In order to create new opportunities abroad that might better suit the underrepresented student populations, to provide more adequate pre-departure and post-return counseling, to better integrate work done abroad with on-campus requirements, and to interest more faculty in study abroad and its students, the committee made a wide-ranging series of recommendations to the university.

Promote philosophical discussion and policy formation concerning the purposes of study abroad. Faculty members seem quite unclear about the aims and benefits of study abroad. While they support the EAP warmly, many do not connect study abroad *academically* with their own disciplines.   Faculty and administrative groups should be asked to discuss in a more focused way what specific objectives the EAP should serve.   The committee hoped that this sort of discussion would be promoted at both the university-wide and local levels, including a system-wide conference at which distinguished university faculty who were knowledgeable about international education would set out a philosophical program for the future.

Involve more faculty members in the discussion of study abroad. Since so many faculty members admit to ignorance about the Education Abroad Program, and others are misguided in thinking there are no academic opportunities suitable for their students abroad, or that study abroad unduly disrupts their students' education, measures should be taken to reach these faculty, educate them about available opportunities, and involve them directly in the EAP.   The current yearly mailings about student and faculty opportunities within the EAP are clearly not an adequate source of information; person-to-person contact would be much more effective.   The faculty committees that oversee the EAP should periodically organize discussions, perhaps on a rotating basis, with those departments whose faculty members are not highly aware, and even with those closely linked to study abroad.   Such discussions should not only seek to educate but should also elicit suggestions and constructive criticism.

Faculty members not usually involved with the EAP should be invited to serve as consultants for the selection of participants or to serve on EAP-related committees.   Returning EAP students in the underrepresented disciplines should be asked to make their faculty advisors more aware of their academic training abroad.

Since faculty members with extensive personal travel experience tend to support study abroad enthusiastically, such people in the underrepresented disciplines should be sought out and involved in planning and recruitment efforts.   Faculty members should be invited to help design the curriculum of new EAP programs, to suggest innovative programs, and to share connections with foreign colleagues who might cooperate in programs.   While there currently exist incentives, such as study center directorships all over the world and research exchange opportunities in the Soviet Union and Pacific Rim countries for a handful of faculty each year, these should be expanded, since faculty with experience in international research and instruction will be the best advocates and advisors in the future.

Enhance the role of study abroad in the core curriculum. International education should become a part of any discussion about modifications to the core curriculum.   The home campus core curriculum may simply not be sufficient in breadth, depth, or rigor to produce the intellectual sophistication and in-depth understanding of cultural differences needed to function in today's world. More programs in which study abroad is an integral part of the undergraduate curriculum should be encouraged.

Target discipline-specific information about opportunities abroad to the faculty. Since faculty members in academic disciplines or subdisciplines that do not have a natural affinity for comparative, humanistic, or linguistic approaches to knowledge now underestimate the course work available abroad to benefit their majors, information about EAP programs should be targeted to faculty in a discipline-specific way, so as to present to each department just those study centers that have excellent faculty and educational opportunities for their students.

Encourage greater flexibility in major and breadth requirements, particularly in highly specialized majors. If study abroad is to become more academically related to certain disciplines, it might be necessary to restructure the requirements for highly specialized majors. For example, students might be allowed to take some major requirements early and to defer some breadth requirements to be completed abroad.

Better publicize opportunities available abroad. Departments should be encouraged to publicize EAP internally. Each department should inform potential students about study abroad opportunities by a statement in the college catalog. Returned EAP students might act as peer advisors for students in their discipline.

Strengthen counseling. Greater emphasis should be paid to counseling on both the departmental and college levels, so as to avoid unduly discouraging students from study abroad and to help students start early in planning a feasible mix of elective, breadth, and major courses integrating study abroad.

Encourage greater participation by minority students. It would be worthwhile to study the complex situation of ethnic minority students with respect to study abroad, in order to discover what effects economic deprivation, choices of major, attitudes toward language learning, and GPA have on minority students' low participation rates. Scholarship opportunities for minorities should be enhanced. Additionally, what incentives might make language learning more attractive to these students?

Improve reintegration of study abroad returnees. More should be done to help returning students readapt to campus life. The EAP students' participation in relevant courses and seminars would both help them relate the academic work done abroad to the general aims of their education and allow them to contribute to the educational goals of the campus. Returning students might be "debriefed" by their departmental advisors in order to assess the articulation of their experience with major programs. Students might participate with faculty committees in discussing the curricular aspects of EAP with the underrepresented disciplines.

Study the long-term impact of study abroad on the student. The long-term effects of study abroad should be assessed by tracking the careers of University of California graduates who participated in EAP. The current evaluation of returnees' EAP experience is extensive and informative, but it occurs only immediately after return and does not capture their long-term growth and judgments. We really do not know how study abroad affects people's lives or how it relates in the long run to advanced study or professional development.

RECENT PROGRESS

The recommendations summarized above were presented to the University during the fall quarter, 1988, and have since been discussed in various administrative offices and faculty committees connected to the Education Abroad Program. Since the University of California is so administratively complex and grants such a large role to faculty opinion, these discussions will be lengthy and will have to encompass a very broad participation if they are to have lasting results. And since the recommendations themselves are wide ranging and are targeted to several different levels of the university—the President's Office, EAP's central administration, individual campuses, colleges, and departments, the relevant committees of the faculty Senate— progress will both take time and will be piecemeal.

A number of recent developments, both directly and indirectly related to the Study Abroad Articulation Project, are currently bringing about an evolution in EAP programming, in EAP's relations with the UC faculty, and in its coordination with the various campus administrative offices. Contemporaneous with the SAAP, two other close examinations of EAP were conducted during 1988. One was an administrative review, examining the current leadership structure, finances, and curricular planning of EAP in advance of the impending search for a new director; the other was a general curricular review sponsored by the appropriate committees of the faculty Academic Senate. All three studies have resulted in compatible recommendations for the future evolution of the EAP's structure and programming and for changes in the ways it articulates with the home campuses. The EAP's new director, a respected UC faculty member with wide international and EAP experience who came into office in January 1990, is placing a high priority on implementing key recommendations of all three reports.

Within EAP's central administration, the Needs Assessment and Program Implementation Committee has created an agenda for action that includes several recommendations of our SAAP report. Among the actions now underway are a pilot project to provide discipline-specific material about opportunities at EAP centers to selected underrepresented disciplines; closer study of the needs of students from the underrepresented disciplines in the planning of new programs abroad; and efforts to identify and involve receptive and knowledgeable faculty members in the underrepresented areas, in order to have expert consultants to promote better planning and recruitment. Additionally, efforts have been stepped up to provide better counseling to potential students and to better articulate the ways in which on-campus student services (such as the registrar, financial aid, the college offices, etc.) provide for the special needs of EAP students.

5

THE UNIVERSITY OF COLORADO AT BOULDER: THE INTERNATIONAL AFFAIRS MAJOR

Jean Delaney

With the assistance of a grant from the Ford Foundation, the Office of International Education began a project in conjunction with seven other American universities to assess and strengthen the articulation between work done on study abroad and the home campus curriculum. At the University of Colorado at Boulder (UCB), a small committee of faculty and staff was created in the spring of 1987 that discussed and identified two issues to address. The committee decided to focus on students majoring in International Affairs (IA) as a pilot project.

The first issue was identified as one of information distribution. An academic advising "catalog" is being compiled that can be used by faculty, staff, and students to assist students in selecting courses applicable to their IA major before they leave Boulder for their study abroad site. With this document, we hope students and faculty members will address the articulation of courses more directly.

The second articulation issue is one of attitudes, goal setting, and assessing academic outcomes. Students returning from a study abroad program frequently comment, "My year abroad was the most rewarding and educational experience of my life, but really all the learning ... did was outside the classroom. The academic work wasn't very important." A certain amount of amazement about how much can be learned outside the classroom is to be expected from students having their first encounter with a foreign culture. The learning that does occur is very powerful, but somehow it is not "academic" in the students' minds. It is clear, however, that students do learn from their course work as well as from their experiences outside the classroom, and this combination is one of the most important aspects of studying abroad. With this is mind, the committee developed the following hypotheses:

1. Students do not recognize the academic value of their overseas experience, in and outside the classroom, because they do not know what their faculty and departments expect them to learn.
2. Students who are aware of their departments' expectations in specific and measurable academic goals will achieve those goals more readily and have a greater understanding and appreciation of the learning they have achieved. Further, those who know these goals prior to going abroad will be better prepared to achieve the goals than those who do not.

We drew up goals statements for international affairs majors studying abroad to make explicit the expectations of the program to the students. The following five goals were approved by the IA Curriculum Committee.

GOALS FOR INTERNATIONAL AFFAIRS MAJORS STUDYING ABROAD

1. To achieve a greater familiarity with the cultural, historical, economic, and social background of the host country and the geographic region than would be available through work in this country.

2. To achieve a firsthand understanding of the issues being debated and decisions being made in the host country.

3. To sensitize the student to differences in the legitimate political objectives of various international actors and recognize possible conflicts with U.S. objectives.

4. To achieve an understanding of the normalcy of ambiguity in international relations.

5. To achieve the ability to converse fluently with the citizens of the host country, read scholarly journals, and do research using original sources.

An assessment test (below) was developed and sent to twenty-four IA majors studying abroad in May 1987. Only one was returned, unfortunately. However, a group of five of these same students was gathered in Boulder on September 26, 1988 to discuss the test and its usefulness. The students had studied abroad in Bordeaux and Chambery, France; Regensburg, Germany; and Seville, Spain. Jean Delaney and Randy Huntsberry conducted the group interview.

Although the number of participants in the discussion was small, the results were encouraging.

- The students were concerned about which courses would apply to their major and felt better advising before departure for their program would be advantageous.
- Courses taken abroad that were applicable to IA gave the students different perspectives than those available in

Boulder. Students were expected to do a great deal more independent research.

- Clearly, extracurricular activities were very important to learning about the country and its political activities. The students cited chances to talk to fellow students, their host families, or people met by chance while traveling.
- The experience of studying international affairs abroad was described as "reality," while studying the same subject in Boulder was only "theoretical."
- Students noted that they were using what they learned abroad in preparing papers for their IA classes this year in Boulder.
- All the students remembered receiving the assessment test and agreed that it helped them recognize just how much they had learned during their time abroad.
- All the students agreed that they were feeling "out of synch" with their academic work in Boulder; classes were too general, too superficial, and too abstract; fellow students seemed shallow and uninformed about the complexity and ambiguity of the wider world. One student observed that she felt she was intimidating her friends with her new knowledge.

Although one cannot report actual results from such a small sample, we do have a good guide for further efforts. The very positive student reaction to the test was encouraging. The students agreed it would be valuable to see the goals and the test before departure.

During orientation for spring 1989 study abroad programs, the ten IA majors who were to participate were given the same assessment without any prior warning. After taking the test, the students discussed what they could do abroad that would help them improve their test results since they would be expected to take the same test in Boulder the following Fall. The results of these pre-and post-program tests will be evaluated and compared by faculty from the IA program.

It is possible that the test will discern gaps in students' knowledge acquired abroad (e.g., economic understanding) or distinguish differences in knowledge and skills acquisition on different programs (e.g., students who study in Bordeaux, France might gain a much more sophisticated understanding of international affairs than those who study in Seville, Spain). However, a much larger group must be involved in the testing before any convincing results can be reported. Our initial problem of participation in the process remains.

In our first distribution of the assessment test, the one that was returned was filled out thoroughly and thoughtfully. A second test, completed by a different student after her return, was done superficially, incompletely, even inaccurately. These might show the gamut of the quality of participation. When the test was given to the next group of students during their pre-departure orientation, they appeared to give the test their attention and best effort. However, an initial reading shows the answers to be remarkably naive and incomplete. The post-program test of this second group of students will be an important indication of how seriously we can involve the students in this type of assessment.

PLANS FOR THE FUTURE AND IMPLICATIONS

During spring, 1989 orientations for fall and academic year programs abroad, we will give IA majors the test. These same students will be sent the same test at the end of their study abroad program, and a comparison will be made between their pre-departure and pre-departure and post-program responses. If we get good participation and measurable results from the ten IA spring semester students, we might consider adding a second large group of majors studying abroad in the 1989 and 1990 project, for example, Spanish majors. To do this, we would need to identify faculty members interested in and willing to work on the goals statements and an assessment activity.

With enough experience, and the possibility of useful results, OIE (Office of International Education) might try to develop a generic or general education set of goals applicable to all students studying abroad. Alternatively, goals for individual programs might be more appropriate.

To address the students' inability to focus on their studies and "articulate"their experiences abroad with those at Boulder, a pilot "reentry course" has been approved for the spring semester, 1989, by the College of Arts and Sciences. This course, ARS–3000 "Journeys Between Self and Other," will offer students returning from abroad an opportunity to analyze the knowledge they gained abroad and its applicability to their academic program at UCB. The course is being taught by Randy Huntsberry, a consultant for the Office of International Education for the 1988 and 1989 academic year. Students will read five pieces of fiction that describe encounters with another culture, discuss the nature of that encounter and how it changes the travelers' perceptions of themselves as well as their perceptions of the foreign culture and their home culture. The readings are Graham Greene, *The Quiet American*; Willa Cather, *Death Comes for the Archbishop*; E.M. Forster, *A Passage to India*; Elenore Smith Bowen, *Return to Laughter*; Joseph Conrad, *Heart of Darkness*.

The development of the course catalog for advising IA majors was a far more difficult and time-consuming project than we anticipated. However, with the catalog, we can plan meetings with IA faculty advisors to explain the use of the catalog and the need for IA majors to be aware of the opportunities to study courses appropriate to their major. After a year of use, we hope to get an evaluation from the faculty as to its usefulness. This will determine whether we should update the catalog annually, expand it to other majors, or abandon the project. Using the catalog, we should have greater access to faculty members and give them a broader understanding of the study abroad programs.

Overseas Activities

The implications for study abroad program design and improvement are very exciting. While these activities were occurring in Boulder, in Denmark, the DIS (Danish International Studies Program), a study abroad program designed for foreign students, became interested in the project. The DIS used the IA goals statements as the basis for a discussion for one of their biannual faculty seminars. Happily, our goals correspond largely with what DIS attempts to teach the students who come to them from over 100 different institutions in three countries. As a result of those discussions, the DIS program will be modified in the following ways:

1. Their student orientation August 1989 will be expanded to include two lectures: one on the history of Denmark, the other on current politics, both foreign and domestic.
2. Orientation materials will include a digest of foreign press coverage on Denmark.
3. Students in political science classes will be expected to read regularly from the *Financial Times*.
4. All DIS students will be given our assessment test at the end of this semester.

The UCB is becoming a member of the DIS program in 1989. The partnership on outcomes assessment is virtually in place already, which promises a great deal of interesting and valuable information for the future and a high quality academic experience for UCB students.

**Goals Statements for International Affairs Majors Studying Abroad
and Assessment Questions**

Program_____

Goal 1:   To achieve a greater familiarity with the cultural, historical, economic, and social background of the host country and the geographic region than would be available through work in this country.

1. What cultural activities have you participated in that are unavailable or unexploited in the United States, for example visiting museums, going to concerts, operas, or plays?

2. Describe your host country's economic position in the world, for example, monetary exchange, trade balance, internal economic health, and where you have learned these issues.

3. What new information/facts/insights have you gained about the history of your host country during this time abroad?

4. What role do women play in your host country's society, for example, percentage of the work force, access to non-traditional jobs, and so on?

Goal 2: To achieve a firsthand understanding of the issues being debated and decisions being made in the host country.

1. List the five most controversial topics being covered in the news of your host country.

2. Name five to ten governmental leaders (national or local), their titles, and general political persuasion.

Goal 3: To sensitize the student to differences in the legitimate political objectives of various international actors (and recognize possible conflicts with U.S. objectives).

1. What is your host country's relationship to the United States (trade agreements, military treaties, general attitude of the government or population)?

2. Name one or two issues in which your host country opposes the U.S. stance and why. (Does the government policy reflect the opinion of the population?)

Goal 4: To achieve an understanding of the normalcy of ambiguity in international relations.

1. What contradictions do you observe in your host country?

2. Describe two different positions held by competing political parties on an issue currently facing your host country.

Goal 5:   To achieve the ability to converse fluently with the citizens of the host country, read scholarly journals, and do research using original sources.

1. Describe a concept that is easily expressed in the language of your host country, but is not easily expressed in English.

2. Name three scholarly works you have read in the host country language (journal articles, primary sources, but not general textbooks) and why (class assignment, for a paper or presentation, etc.).

Goal 6:   To develop critical thinking and an ability to reason.

1. Name up to three assumptions that you held by virtue of your American background, that have been challenged by your stay in your host country. (These could be personal, political, social, or economic).

2. Have you been engaged in a discussion, in class or out, that has challenged a belief or opinion you hold? Please describe the issue, the situation, and the results.

Please feel free to add any other comments or observations that you think relate to your achievement of the goals as listed above.

6

POMONA COLLEGE: FACTORS INFLUENCING STUDENTS' DECISIONS TO STUDY ABROAD

Cecilia Cloughly

The Study Abroad Articulation Project (SAAP) funded by the Ford Foundation provided an opportunity for Pomona College to step back from the ongoing effort of sending approximately 50% of its student body abroad in order to analyze the history of study abroad at the college since the 1950s. The full report written in 1987 brought together for the first time statistics concerning the number of students abroad and their destinations. The tables and charts compiled from these statistics revealed trends and valuable information about the impact of various college policies in effect over the years.

The second part of the Pomona College Ford Project was to try to determine if and how the number of students going abroad in underrepresented majors might be increased. Faculty members and administrators had anecdotal evidence about reasons students supposedly decide against studying abroad. The Task Force sponsored a questionnaire answered by 84.3% of the 1987 graduating seniors who did not study abroad under Pomona College's auspices. Had the survey revealed that general education requirements were a major stumbling block preventing students from going abroad, the Task Force was prepared to take the issue to the faculty. However, the survey revealed that class scheduling—not general education requirements—is the most significant barrier. In addition, the survey indicated that the number of students who had not already had a significant experience abroad and who wanted to do so is actually quite small. Thus, it appears that the college has been successful through its extensive offerings and financial aid to serve the majority of its potential participants.

During 1987-1988 and 1988-1989 increased efforts at articulation with certain departments, some policy changes, an increase in the size of the entering classes, and the application of the recommendations of the 1987 full SAAP report all contributed programs in fourteen countries: the People's Republic of China, the Dominican Republic, England, France, West Germany, Greece, Israel, Italy, Japan, Nepal, Scotland, Spain, Sweden, and Switzerland.   Only 5% were on non-Pomona programs, where students had academic reasons to select a program sponsored by another institution.   Of the May 1987 graduates, 144 (45%) had studied abroad for Pomona College credit.   In 1987-1988, students selected from over forty options in sixteen countries.

The Office of International Education is administered by a staff of four full-time employees: a director, an associate director, an administrative assistant, and a secretary.   The director reports to the vice president for academic affairs.   All policy matters are decided by the International Education Committee, whose faculty chair provides a valuable liaison with the faculty.

International Majors—One of Every Eight Students

One of every eight seniors in the class of 1987 pursued a major with a significant international component—Anthropology, Asian studies, Chinese, foreign languages, foreign literature, French, German, international relations, linguistics, and Spanish.

International relations (known as IR on campus) is one of the college's most popular majors; it ranks sixth in size among the departments.   This challenging multidisciplinary major requires its students to complete six semesters in one language or four semesters in each of two languages.   International relations students are normally expected to live at least one semester in the Oldenborg Center and to spend a semester abroad.

The Department of Modern Languages and Literatures has more than twice as many faculty members as any other department.   Enrollment patterns are healthy;   total departmental enrollments for the 1986-1987 academic year were 1,415, a 9.8% increase over the 1,288 enrollment figure for the previous year.   About half of the approximately 1,250 students on campus are enrolled in language classes each semester. Eighteen students graduated in 1987 with majors in the department.   The number of graduating seniors majoring in languages and linguistics at Pomona College has more than tripled from five in 1975 to eighteen in 1987.   This contrasts favorably with the national trend, where the number of students majoring in foreign languages decreased almost 50% between 1975 and 1985.

Pomona College requires three semesters of a foreign language or equivalent proficiency for graduation and offers eleven language options: Mandarin Chinese, French, German, classical Greek, modern Greek, Biblical Hebrew, modern Hebrew, Japanese, Latin, Russian, and Spanish.   In addition, students may take Italian at one of the other Claremont Colleges.

Asian studies is rapidly growing as a major at Pomona College. This interdisciplinary major combines requirements in an Asian language and area studies. Pomona College's long-standing connections with the Far East make this an exciting program for students. Enrollments in Japanese and Chinese are increasing each year.

The Oldenborg Center for Modern Languages and International Relations

This dormitory and program facility houses 137 students each semester, providing about one-eighth of on-campus accommodations. Students are assigned to the Chinese, French, German, Japanese, Russian, or Spanish section. The center offers a number of activities to the campus as a whole, including conversation classes taught by the six foreign-born language residents, an active series of lectures in international relations, and luncheon language tables featuring twenty-one different languages. The six "Oldenborg" languages meet daily; at present, tables for fifteen other languages meet once or twice a week: American Sign Language, Arabic, Armenian, Dutch, Greek, Hindi-Urdu, Italian, Korean, Norwegian, Portuguese, Serbo-Croatian, Swedish, Tagalog, Thai, and Vietnamese.

Because the luncheon language tables and conversation classes at the Oldenborg Center provide a relatively easy way to maintain skills in one foreign language while learning another, Pomona College has an unusually high number of students learning a second (or even third) foreign language. Students majoring in languages are normally expected to live at least one semester in the Oldenborg Center and to spend a semester abroad.

Foreign-Born Students at Pomona College

During 1986-1987 eighty foreign-born students attended Pomona College. Of these, twenty-two were visa holders and fifty-eight were permanent residents with the option of becoming United States citizens in due course. International students represent 6% of the college's enrollment.

STUDY ABROAD POLICIES AS OF 1986-1987

Credit

Because the study abroad experience is considered an integral part of the academic program, the college requires all students seeking academic credit for work done abroad to obtain prior approval from the International Education Committee, an interdisciplinary faculty group with two returned students as voting members. No credit is granted retroactively for work done abroad during the academic year while a student is on leave from the institution.

Eligibility and Minimum GPA Requirement

Over three-fourths (77%) of the students enrolled at Pomona College are eligible for study abroad by meeting the minimum cumulative GPA set by the International Education Committee— 8.5, or 2.83 on the four-point scale. (The college has a twelve-point scale with A and A+ as 12.0.) In addition, students who are required to study abroad by their majors (anthropology, Asian studies, international relations, and modern languages) and who do not meet the minimum GPA may do so, if they have the support of their departments and can demonstrate convincing academic reasons why they cannot postpone the experience until they are able to meet the minimum GPA (Beginning in 1988, the International Education Committee decided to accept applications from any student in good standing. All students are evaluated on the basis of a number of criteria, including recent academic performance, preparation, and demonstrated motivation.)

Equalized Fee Structure and Financial Aid Policy

The International Education Committee eliminated the monetary incentive to choose non-Pomona programs by making the cost for all study programs abroad the same as that on campus, effective in 1985-1986.

The changed fee structure is consistent with the college's policy of equal opportunity for students of differing financial means. Furthermore, this "flat-fee" policy is the logical extension of the principle of the "need-blind" admissions policy for entering students to which the college has long subscribed, that is, students are admitted to the college without consideration of financial need, and financial aid packages are calculated only after admissions decisions are reached. Finally, the principle of having students on differing programs abroad pay the same amount for the Pomona College credit parallels the campus policy of charging the same, no matter what courses the student takes or where he or she lives. Thus, students in more costly on-campus programs (such as the sciences) or programs abroad (in Japan, for example) are subsidized by students in programs with lower expenses. Likewise, students on financial aid are subsidized to a certain extent by those students who are not on financial aid (and governmental taxes paid by the parents of non-financial aid students).

Students on financial aid receive the same allowance abroad as they would in Claremont for either a Pomona program or a non-Pomona one, although work/study components of financial aid packages are replaced by loans. Travel expenses are equalized because the college provides all students an allowance equal to round-trip transportation from Los Angeles to the site abroad.

Non-Pomona Programs

If a student has good academic reasons to go on a program other than one sponsored by Pomona College, the International Education Committee grants permission for the student to do so. (The percentage of students on non-Pomona programs declined from 45% in 1984-1985 to 4.6% in 1986-1987.) Faculty members evaluate the work brought back by students on non-Pomona programs for credit.

Encouragement of Study Abroad Outside of Europe

Following the mandate of the 1983-1984 Task Force, the International Education Committee intensified efforts to suggest to students that they might consider programs outside of Europe, especially in developing countries. New Pomona programs were identified in Nepal and in the Dominican Republic. A counseling folder on programs in the Third World was prepared and made available to students. The percentage of students studying outside of Europe more than tripled from a low of 8% in 1984-1985 to 28% in 1986-1987. The number of students going to Africa has recently jumped since new campus courses in African studies have been added to the curriculum.

Encouragement of the Study of a Foreign Language

Since the number studying in Great Britain peaked in 1984-1985 at 40%, the number of students there has decreased to approximately 25%. Since some Pomona programs require students to begin studying a foreign language, about 75%-80% of the students abroad are learning a foreign language.

Calculation of the Grade Point Average

The grades received on Pomona programs abroad are calculated into the college's GPA. Grades from non-Pomona programs appear on the transcript but are not included in the Pomona College GPA.

Timing of the Study Abroad Experience

Students may go abroad during the second semester of the sophomore year, the junior year, or the first semester of the senior year. On occasion, students petition to go during the first semester of the sophomore year and the second semester of the senior year. Because some faculty members and administrators are concerned that the exodus for study abroad of such a large portion of the junior class has deleterious effects on campus life and the curriculum, students are encouraged to consider going either during the second semester of the sophomore year or the first semester of the senior year. Specifically, programs for completing the third semester of the foreign language requirement have been made available.

Major Requirements

Students may receive credit toward major requirements if they obtain prior tentative approval from the department chair of the major. The amount of credit to be granted toward the major is determined by the department chair after the student returns and presents the work done abroad for evaluation. In practice, many students are allowed to fulfill major requirements with work done abroad.

Foreign Language and General Education Requirements

Students may use courses abroad to fulfill the foreign language requirement but not general education requirements.

Numerical Balance Between Fall and Spring Semester

Because Pomona College is a residential college housing 96% of its students on campus, the balance between the number of students off campus in fall and spring is crucial. Since, for a number of reasons, students prefer to be away during the fall, the International Education Committee must encourage spring participation by planning attractive spring programs in an ongoing effort to balance the numbers between semester as evenly as possible.

Summer Study Abroad

The college does not have a summer term on campus, nor does it sponsor any summer programs abroad. Beginning with summer 1987 the Office of International Education assumed the responsibility of facilitating the selection of summer abroad opportunities and the awarding of credit.

Because study abroad programs are not accredited by an independent outside agency, students wishing to receive credit for summer study abroad must obtain prior tentative approval from the appropriate faculty member(s). A maximum of two courses credit may be awarded upon the recommendation of faculty members who evaluate the work presented by students upon their return to campus.

THE SCOPE OF THE RESEARCH PROJECT

A preliminary study showed that 58% of the eligible students in the class of 1987 took advantage of Pomona College's Education Abroad Program. What are the reasons behind the individual decisions of the 42% who did not go abroad? Over the years staff members in the Office of International Education have heard a variety of reasons for students' failing to follow through on an initial interest in study abroad.

It seemed a worthwhile goal for the Ford Articulation Project Task Force to examine the relative importance of the reasons eligible students do not study abroad and to ask questions in three areas of concern.

1. Who Are the Students Who Don't Study Abroad?
   - What are their majors?
   - Are they men or women?
   - What are their GPA's?
   - Have they already had a significant experience abroad (lived, studied, or merely traveled)?

2. Why Do Students Decide Not to Study Abroad?
   - What is the relative importance of the various reasons?
   - Which students are affected by these reasons?

3. Should Policy, Programmatic, or Scheduling Changes Be Made?
   - Should the International Education Committee increase its negotiations with individual departments about scheduling conflicts with certain required courses?
   - Should students be allowed to use certain courses abroad to fulfill general education requirements?
   - Should students be encouraged to consider summer study abroad experiences if they cannot be away from campus for a semester or a year?

IDENTIFICATION OF THE TARGET GROUP

With the excellent cooperation of Pomona College Registrar Monica Augustin, statistics about the class of 1987 in regard to participation in Pomona's study abroad program and eligibility based on meeting a minimum GPA were developed. Since this research was conducted in the spring of the senior year, the numbers could not be exact because some students delayed graduation and others had incomplete or pending grades. Nonetheless, the relative percentages are accurate.

The preliminary study included 319 Pomona College seniors, of whom 247 (77%) qualified by meeting the 8.5 cumulative minimum GPA set by the International Education Committee. Four groups of students were identified:

Seniors who have studied abroad (45%). The 145 students who chose to study for a semester or year for academic credit at Pomona College make up this group. They represent 45% of the graduating class or 58% of the eligible seniors.

Target group (32%). The Target group consists of 102 students who met the minimum GPA requirement and chose not to study a semester or year abroad.

Marginal GPA (9%). The twenty-nine students whose GPAs were marginal, that is probably below 8.5 at the time they would have applied for a study abroad program, did not receive a questionnaire.

GPA below the established minimum (14%). The forty-four students whose overall grade point averages were below the minimum required by the International Education Committee (8.5, or 2.83 on the four-point scale) were placed in this group. The questionnaire was not sent to these ineligible students.

THE QUESTIONNAIRE

A rough draft of a questionnaire addressed to the seniors who were eligible but chose not to study abroad was reviewed by the Ford Articulation Project Task Force, which consisted of representatives from all three teaching divisions: from the college's international programs the Curriculum Committee and the administration. Two members of the Sociology Department made additional refinements in the questionnaire and assisted in using the SPSS statistics program on the college's IBM mainframe to analyze the results. Graphs were produced with the Excel program on a Macintosh personal computer.

The number-coded questionnaires (Figure 1) were sent out shortly before graduation in envelopes from the office of

Academic Vice-President Jerry Irish. The questionnaire's brevity, the anonymous response format, and official stationery resulted in an unusually high response rate (84.3%). The GPAs, majors, and female/male distribution of the sixteen non-respondents were examined; they are representative of the target group as a whole.

CHARACTERISTICS OF THE TARGET GROUP

Female/Male Distribution

Given that the Pomona College senior class is almost equally divided between women (52%) and men (48%), it might be expected that the students abroad would have the same gender distribution. However, Pomona College students abroad are predominantly female (61% women, 39% men).

A preponderance of women is a common phenomenon in most programs abroad nationwide. The Council on International Educational Exchange reported that 65% of the holders of International Student Identification Cards in 1983-1984 were women.   There is evidence indicating that this two-to-one female/male ratio has been consistent over the years. By this measure, Pomona College's study abroad programs include a few more men than the national average would predict.

Since so many more women went abroad than men, it might be expected that the target group would contain significantly more men than women. However, this turned out not to be the case; 52.3% are male, 47.7% female.

By Division

Overall in the college, the largest group of students (slightly less than half) major in the social sciences division. About one third of the students are in the sciences and about one fourth in the humanities.

Of the students who went abroad during 1986-1987, 28% are in the humanities, 65% in the social sciences, and 7% in the sciences.

The target group also has more students in the social sciences (44%) than in the sciences (37%). Only 19% of the targeted group is in the humanities.

By Major

Students abroad by major. Four of the over twenty majors offered at Pomona College require a study abroad experience: anthropology, Asian studies, international relations, and modern languages. Small percentages of the science students go abroad biology 9%, physics 13%; chemistry 20%; mathematics 24%; and geology 40%).   Some social science majors are not well represented: psychology (29%), economics (31%), history (37%), government (38%), and public policy analysis (44%).

Target Group by Major. Biology, mathematics, physics, psychology, government, public policy analysis, and economics majors are most highly represented among the qualified students who chose not to go abroad. These majors also have a relatively large number of major requirements. Public policy analysis, in particular, is an interdisciplinary program with a required three-semester sequence (class/internship/thesis), which makes it difficult for its majors to go abroad during their last three semesters of study.

By GPA

Target group by GPA Approximately one half of the students (51%) in the target group had GPAs between 9.0 and 10.0; 35% had GPAs between 10.0 and 11.0. Only 14% were over 11.0. The average GPA of the target group was 10.09, and the median GPA was 10.00.

Students abroad by GPA The statistics for the group that studied abroad are similar to those for the target group, when the groups are made comparable by eliminating the students who were allowed to go abroad despite a GPA below the minimum. The statistics for the total study abroad group show an average GPA of 9.98 and a median of 10.05.

The similarity in the GPA statistics provides evidence that factors other than GPA influence the decision about who does or does not go abroad.

RESULTS OF THE QUESTIONNAIRE

As indicated in Figure 1, the possible reasons for not studying abroad included:
1. Class scheduling conflicts
2. Conflicts with major requirements
3. Preference for campus activity
4. Previous experience abroad
5. No interest
6. Lack of program appeal
7. Concern about personal expenses abroad
8. Desire for more courses on campus for graduate study
9. Separation from friends
10. Difficulty in fulfilling general education requirements
11. Preference for a domestic program

12. Dislike of foreign languages
13. GPA below the established minimum
14. Application deadlines
15. Family objections
16. Concern about terrorism or personal safety
17. Fear of lowering GPA
18. Health reasons

The primary two reasons by "importance"—"Class scheduling conflicts" and "Could not fulfill major requirements abroad"— were named more than twice as many times as the next two reasons: "Preference for a campus activity" and "Previous experience abroad" (Figure 2).

The order of the reasons is slightly altered in Figure 3 where students have indicated that a given reason had at least a little importance in the decision not to go abroad. In the "relevance" rankings, the top four reasons are the same as the "importance" ranking. "Difficulty in fulfilling general education requirements" moves up from tenth to fifth place. "Friends" seem to play a more important role, and "terrorism" and "dislike of foreign languages" increase in significance.

Class Scheduling Conflicts

"Scheduling conflict with classes needed or wanted" was the reason most often selected by the target group (66 students or 77%). Students in the science division have the most difficulty with scheduling conflicts (83.9%). Nonetheless, more than half of the social sciences (64.8%) and humanities (56.3%) students feel that "scheduling conflict" was at least "of some importance" to their decision.

Over 50% (and, in several majors, 100%) of the students in twenty-one majors report that difficulty in scheduling classes was "very important" or "of some importance" in their decision not to go abroad. Granted, the number of students in each major is small, so one or two students with scheduling problems can affect the percentages significantly. Nonetheless, scheduling appears to be problematic in almost all majors. It is likely that most of these conflicts are with courses required for the major.

Cross-tabulation indicates that the class scheduling problem is of concern to all students, regardless of their GPA

Are there steps the task force might take to ameliorate the situation? Unfortunately, the task force has no control over several factors that often cause students to have scheduling conflicts:

Irregularly taught courses. Many courses, especially advanced ones, are offered only once a year—in the fall or spring. In some smaller departments, courses needed for the major are taught in alternate years.

Faculty members away from campus. Pomona College has generous sabbatical and leave plans for faculty members. Although the college sometimes hires a part-time instructor or a sabbatical replacement, some classes are not held until the absent professor returns to campus. Each year a significant percentage of faculty members is away from campus. For example, 11% of the 135 member faculty were off campus in fall 1987.

Single section classes. Because the college has a small student/faculty ratio (approximately 10:1), many classes have only one section. Sometimes students have a scheduling conflict with two classes being offered at the same time and must delay taking one of them. The college attempts to spread classes over all of the time slots, but many classes are still held at the popular time slots, 9 to 12 on Monday, Wednesday, and Friday.

Impacted classes. Some departments, especially economics and government, are impacted, with waiting lists in popular and required courses. Two particularly problematic classes are "United States Foreign Policy" (Government 155) and "Introduction to International Relations" (Government 64). Because they are core courses for the international relations major, the college is reluctant to entrust these important classes to part-time instructors. Students wanting to go abroad need to take these classes as early as possible but are sometimes placed on waiting lists.

Declaring a major late or changing majors. Many students entering the college are "undeclared majors;" many others change majors, often as late as the junior year. It is a common phenomenon at the college to have an outstanding student graduating in the humanities or social sciences who came to college as a "pre-med" student and eventually majored in a non-science subject. Students who settle on a major late or change majors often have difficulties in scheduling.

Transfer students. Transfer students often do not study abroad because they have difficulties scheduling all of the various requirements. Pomona programs abroad (but not non-Pomona programs) can be used, however, to fulfill the four-semester residency requirement.

Difficulty in Fulfilling Major Requirements

• Two-thirds of the students in the target group think that difficulty in fulfilling major requirements affected their decision not to go abroad.

• Students with higher GPAs place more importance on the conflict between choosing to study abroad and fulfilling major requirements than do students with lower grades. This attitude suggests that some of the better students decide to stay on campus to take a major requirement at Pomona rather than to study abroad and perhaps fulfill the requirement in an alternative way.

• Students in the sciences give more importance to this problem than do the students in the other divisions. The two students with special majors (with more than the average number of major requirements) placed importance on this conflict.

• Students majoring in economics (0%), English (20%), public policy analysis (38%), and psychology (44%) appear to have low conflict with major courses. Yet, relatively small percentages of students in these majors go abroad. In one case, public policy analysis, the stumbling block to going abroad is the required internship. The chair of the Economics Department believes that the strong vocational bent of his majors sometimes prevents them from being more adventurous in their endeavors. The SAAP survey identified underrepresented departments with which articulation discussions might result in an increase in the number going abroad.

Major:	Majors Abroad: %	Conflicts: %	Reporting:
Art	40	0	2
Classics	33	100	1
Economics	31	0	6
English	40	20	5
Government	38	50	8
History	37	50	2
Music	29	67	3
Public Policy	50	38	8
Psychology	29	44	9
Sociology	29	0	1
Theater	14	50	2

Wanted More Courses on Campus for Graduate Study

About one fourth of the students, especially those preparing for graduate study, prefer to take courses on campus that will relate directly to their future plans rather than to spend a semester abroad taking classes of a more generalized nature. This factor overlaps with "difficulty in fulfilling major requirements."

Difficulty with General Education Requirements

Pomona College requires every student to complete a number of general education requirements: two writing-intensive courses; three semesters of foreign language or an equivalent proficiency; and nine "breadth of study" courses, three in each division.

Beginning with the class of 1990, all students must also take a freshman seminar.

Difficulty with general education requirements. Only one third of the target group students stated that "difficulty in fulfilling general education requirements" was a reason why they didn't study abroad.

GPA and general education requirements. Students with high GPA's seem to have fewer problems with the general education requirements than do those with lower marks.

General education requirements by division and major. Science students attach significantly more importance to the conflict with general education requirements than do students in other divisions.   Majors in which students report significant difficulty with fulfilling the general education requirements are biology, chemistry, and physics because of sequential year-long requirements in the major.

Retention of general education requirement policy. Changing the policy to allow general education requirements to be fulfilled by courses abroad would not make it possible for more students to study abroad; the SAAP survey shows that a more significant (and intractable) problem is with major requirements.   There is considerable overlap between "difficulty in fulfilling general education requirements" and "difficulty in fulfilling major requirements." In fact, the cross-tabulation of the two questions shows that only two students who had difficulty with general education requirements did not have them with major requirements.

Furthermore, there would be difficulty in identifying specific courses abroad as "general education" courses. Pomona College students were on twenty-seven different programs during 1986-1987.   Since not every program could have such a course designated, it would be inequitable for those students in the smaller programs.

Previous Experience Abroad

Of the eighty-six respondents, thirty-one in the target group have either traveled, studied, or lived abroad. Of these thirty-one students who have been abroad previously, the majority (55%) have actually lived abroad.   Most of these students are either immigrants or students in the United States on a visa.

Pomona College must question the efficacy of making major policy changes in the hope of enlarging the study abroad group, when the absolute numbers are so small.   There were only thirty-eight qualified students in the senior class who had some interest in going abroad and who had no previous experience abroad.

Preference for Campus Activity

Almost half of the students in the target group (42%) chose a campus activity over study abroad. Sports, internships/jobs, and music are the leading reasons why some students choose to stay in Claremont. Humanities students (62.6%) are more likely to be involved in campus activities than those in the social sciences (40.5%) and the sciences (29.1%). Internships are almost all in the social sciences, but music and sports attract students in all three divisions. These distinctions between divisions in regard to campus activities is yet another indication of the greater level of vocationalism among science and social science students in contrast to humanities students.

Preference for a Domestic Program

Of the fourteen students who indicated that they did something in the United States instead of studying abroad, one half were transfer students. The most popular domestic program attracting students is the Pomona/Swarthmore Exchange Program. Of the six students on domestic exchange, all were women majoring in a science or social science.

No Interest

A third of the students (30 or 35%) responded "I just wasn't interested." The students giving this response were mainly those who also marked "difficulty in fulfilling major requirements," "previous experience abroad," and "no program appealed to me."

Lack of Program Appeal

One-third of the students also reported "no program appealed to me." These students are the same ones who are concerned about fulfilling major requirements and taking additional classes on campus.

Separation from Friends

About a third (34.9%) of the students in the target group attach "relevance" to the reason of not wanting a separation from friends. For example, some students are reluctant to become separated from a particularly close friend, if he or she is not going abroad at the same time to the same or a nearby program. In fact, many of our students apply to the same program with a close friend. Students often travel together before or after a program. Also, students sometimes visit each other during vacation periods.
Some researchers in the field of study abroad believe that friends are the most important reason why students select a

particular program.   Conversely, it is logical that one might
choose not to study abroad if one's close friends do not.

Concern about Personal Expenses Abroad

Over one third of the students are concerned about personal
expenses abroad. Although Pomona College evens out the program
costs among different sites and provides overseas transportation,
students are told that they should budget significantly more
money for personal expenses abroad than they would need in
Claremont.   While abroad, students spend more on vacation
travel, clothes, postage, telephone bills, and entertainment.   As
the dollar's value drops abroad, staff members of the Office of
International Education receive more complaints from students
about the cost of being abroad.

Dislike of Foreign Languages

Extent of dislike of foreign languages. Almost one fifth (18.6%)
of the target group reported disliking foreign languages to some
degree.   Of these sixteen students, nine were male and seven
female.

This phenomenon of dislike of (or difficulty with or fear of)
foreign languages is common among Americans in general.   In
fact, the majority of American students studying abroad are in
Great Britain.   Many of these students admit that the lack of the
necessity to speak a foreign language was a significant reason for
their choice of Great Britain as a study site.

In regard to summer study, the absence of a foreign language
component is even more important; forty-five percent of the
possible summer sites suggested by students in the target group are
in English-speaking countries.

Students not liking foreign languages by division. Almost 26%
of the science students in the target group report disliking foreign
languages (as compared to 12.6% of the humanities students and
16.2% of the social sciences students).

Dislike for foreign languages and high GPA One finding is
puzzling: although the percentage of the total target group that
reports disliking foreign languages is 18.6%, 42% of the students
in the highest GPA category reported some degree of relevance for
"don't like foreign languages."   One suspects that the presence of
highly   motivated   science   students   in   these   two   achieving
subgroups accounts for the higher percentage reporting a dislike
for foreign languages.   Also, one can not help speculating that
fears of not succeeding in foreign languages (and possibly lowering
a high GPA) play a role in this phenomenon.

Experience abroad and dislike of foreign languages. Another
noteworthy correlation is that between a lack of previous
experience abroad and a dislike for foreign languages.   Of the

sixteen students in the target group who acknowledged some degree of dislike for foreign languages, only one had studied or lived abroad, and only two had traveled abroad.

People who dislike foreign languages may be less likely to go abroad in the first place. However, a significant experience abroad (perhaps more than just travel) may have a positive influence on one's view of foreign languages.

Missed Application Deadlines

Only seven students replied that they had missed application deadline(s). These students all had marked other reasons as being more important in the decision. One can assume that no student was really turned away because of a missed deadline. Each semester the International Education Committee accepts one or two late applications, depending upon the circumstances.

Family Objections

Although only a small percentage of students (11%) report family objections to going abroad, it can be assumed that this reason is a significant one. No matter how attractive or relevant the college makes its study abroad offerings, it can also be assumed that serious family objections will prevent the student from going abroad, especially since the student faces higher personal expenses abroad than in Claremont. An analysis of the responses of the ten students who had families with objections shows that six are female and four male. Half or five also indicated a concern about expenses.

Concern for Terrorism and Personal Safety

Only eight students (4 female, 4 male) or 9% of the respondents thought that "concern about terrorism or personal safety" was relevant to their decision not to study abroad.

From this study and from enrollment patterns over the past three years, it seems that fear of terrorism has a stronger effect on timing and site of study than on the decision to participate. For example, after several terrorist incidents in France in 1986, student enrollments in French programs, especially in Paris, declined. However, overall enrollments did not decrease much since students applied to other sites away from the then current "hot spots."

GPA Below the Established Minimum

Only 8% of the target group reported that they thought their GPA was too low. (In order to avoid unnecessarily reminding students of their low GPA, the task force did not send questionnaires to students with senior GPAs below 9.0.)

Fear of Lowering GPA

This factor is not a decisive one; each of the four students (6% of the target group) listed several additional reasons why they chose not to go abroad. Furthermore, three of the four students concerned about the possibility of lowering their GPAs are science majors, who were probably worried about graduate or medical school admission. The fourth student was president of the senior class.

Health Reasons

Although only 5% of the students report health reasons as a decisive factor, this reason is obviously one that no Pomona College efforts will change. However, the institution has always made every effort possible to send abroad motivated students who have handicaps, including blind and functionally deaf students.

CONCLUSIONS

Some Students Cannot or Do Not Want to Study Abroad

Some students just do not want to study abroad for one or more very valid reasons. Others cannot go because of some factor that cannot be changed. In some cases, the deterrents are academic, such as unavoidable class scheduling conflicts and majors with sequential requirements. Other students have compelling personal reasons: close friends, financial problems, previous experience abroad, family objections, health reasons, and so forth.

No Need to Change General Education Requirements

Since the study shows that difficulty in fulfilling general education requirements is not a crucial factor in the decision to go abroad, it is not necessary to convince the faculty to allow courses abroad to fulfill general education requirements.

Non-Feasibility of Pomona Summer Programs Abroad

Although some fifty students (58%) in the target group state that they might have considered participating in a Pomona College summer program if one had been available, it does not seem feasible for Pomona College to consider establishing summer programs abroad. The cost of providing financial aid for equal access to all students is prohibitive. Also, student interests in site and type of program are so diverse that problems would arise if Pomona College sponsored only one or two summer programs.

Vacation Study Abroad, a reference book published by the Institute of International Education, lists over 1,000 summer programs in over eighty countries. It seems unnecessary for Pomona College to attempt to duplicate these efforts.

In 1986-1987 the Office of International Education assumed the new responsibility of facilitating student selection of good summer opportunities, including work, internship, and volunteer programs. Procedures have been developed for students to obtain prior approval for proposed summer work. Credit is determined by faculty evaluation after the students return to campus.

Partially as a result of the SAAP survey, the college increased its attempt to obtain funding for summer scholarships. A grant from the Mellon Foundation and a private scholarship fund are now providing summer scholarships for study abroad for students of Chinese, Japanese, Russian, and Spanish.

Necessity of Broad Access to Study Abroad

The Education Abroad Program serves approximately half of the Pomona College student body. The college's policy of providing round-trip transportation and the same financial aid package as the student would receive on campus makes it possible for students with differing financial means to study abroad, since all but personal expenses are equalized among the various programs. The dollar amount of grant and median grant for the students abroad during 1986-1987 were essentially the same as the comparable figures for the campus as a whole. The percentage of students abroad on financial aid (51%) was very nearly the same as the percentage for the total student body (50%).

Class Scheduling Difficulties on Campus

Campus scheduling difficulties, especially with major requirements, appear to be the major cause of the enrollment imbalance between the semesters. Many students do not have a choice of going abroad in the spring; they must go abroad in the fall or not at all.

RECOMMENDATIONS AND RESULTS OF THE SAAP PROJECT

Creation of New Spring Options

New spring programs in Cambridge, Glasgow, and New Zealand were added to entice students from the fall to the spring, thereby helping to balance the numbers between the two semesters.

Similar Programs Available in Both Fall and Spring

Whenever possible, the International Education Committee has paired similar programs by semester. For example, programs in Edinburgh and Glasgow are offered in the fall and spring respectively. Students interested in a program with no foreign language prerequisite may choose between the fall Athens program or the spring Lund program.

Fulfillment of Major Requirements Abroad

The Office of International Education has facilitated the possibility of students going abroad by devising a prescreening method for departments to examine proposed courses students might take to fulfill a major requirement. In practice, many students are able to fulfill one or more major requirements abroad.

Worldwide Opportunities

In 1986-1987 the College had students in over forty programs in sixteen countries, and more than a fourth of the students abroad were studying outside of Europe.

Articulation with Departments about Program Content

There have been extensive discussions with individual faculty members and department chairs about selecting or creating courses abroad appropriate for major credit, such as a theater option in London, science classes at Queen Mary College and the University of Glasgow, anthropology programs in Third World countries and New Zealand, and economics classes in several countries.

Articulation with Departments about Class Scheduling

Some departments have made scheduling changes that make it easier for some of their majors to study abroad. For example, three music majors were abroad during fall 1987 because the Music Department agreed to teach a required alternate-year fall course during the previous spring. The International Relations Committee has made the course scheduling of the IR curriculum more flexible, thereby allowing students who plan ahead to study abroad either in the fall or in the spring.

Increase in Student Counseling, Especially of Freshmen

The key to solving some scheduling difficulties is early planning—the earlier the better. The Office of International Education plans to intensify its efforts to advise students to plan a block of time for a semester abroad in their four-year schedule while they are in their freshman year.

The Office of International Education holds special information meetings for entering students at least twice a year. Each fall all faculty members receive information about the college's current study abroad offerings. Reports are made from time to time when appropriate to the faculty, to the department chairs, and to the trustees. As a follow-up to the Ford Project, a section about study abroad was added to the official handbook for advisors to encourage the possibility of a study abroad semester or year in early curriculum planning.

Encouragement of Summer Academic and Work Programs

Since it appears that some students for one reason or another feel that they cannot or do not want to be away from campus for a semester, studying abroad for a shorter period of time is an alternative. By facilitating the flow of information and obtaining of academic credit through the Office of International Education, it may be possible for at least some of these students to have a meaningful study abroad experience. In addition, scholarships for foreign language study abroad during the summer are crucial to making this possibility a reality for some deserving students.

The Importance of Flexibility and Variety

In contrast to schools that send a small percentage of their students abroad for a year, Pomona College has chosen to facilitate study abroad for shorter time periods, thus enabling a very high percentage to study abroad for one semester or during the summer.

The current policies of the International Education Committee are flexible in regard to:
- Length of time abroad (year, semester, or summer)
- Timing of abroad experience (sophomore, junior, or senior year)
- Type of experience (wide program variation—54 options in 1987-88)
- Level of foreign language proficiency needed to study abroad
- Site of program (26 locations in 16 countries in 1987-88)
- Possibility of obtaining major credit for work abroad

• Availability of "non-Pomona" status for those students
  needing special programs

AFTERWORD

Pomona College is grateful to the Ford Foundation for
financially supporting the survey and the task force. The project
has provided an opportunity for the institution to analyze what it
is already doing and to assess its options for increasing
articulation between the college's extensive study abroad programs
and its curriculum. Although the SAAP task force recognizes the
inherent problems in interpreting questionnaire responses from a
relatively small number of students from one class, the survey has
been extremely helpful in clarifying some issues for the college.
The substantial increase in the number of students abroad during
1988-1989 and the creation of new summer scholarship
opportunities are tangible results partially stimulated by the
Study Abroad Articulation Project.

Many people assisted in the project, but special
acknowledgement should be made to Professors Richard Sheirich
and Hans Palmer, who have both served as chair of the
International Education Committee during the project.

Figure 1. QUESTIONNAIRE AND RESULTS
(Percentage responding printed in bold below question)

TO: Selected Graduating Seniors Who Did Not Study abroad
From: Faculty Task Force for the Ford Foundation Articulation
            Project on Study Abroad in the Curriculum

We are trying to learn why students do or do not study abroad for a semester or year during their years at Pomona College. Please return to the Vice-President's Office in the enclosed envelope by **Tuesday, May 5, 1987. Thank you.**

Indicate the relative importance of each reason in your decision not to study abroad by circling V, S,L, or N:

> **V: VERY important**
> **S: SOME importance**
> **L: LITTLE importance**
> **N: NOT relevant at all**

1. V   S   L   N   Circle: Already traveled/ lived/ studied/ abroad
   12   16   8   64%   **35%   55%**
   10% of respondents

2. V   S   L   N   Scheduling conflict with classes needed or wanted.
   48   23   6   23%

3. V   S   L   N   Couldn't fulfill major requirements abroad.
   36   20   12   33%

4. V   S   L   N   Couldn't fulfill General Education requirements abroad
   6   9   22   63%

5. V   S   L   N   Wanted more sources on campus for graduate study.
   7   11   9   73%

6. V   S   L   N   Didn't want to take a chance on lowering my G.P.A.
   1   0   5   94%

7. V   S   L   N   My G.P.A. was not high enough.
   1   5   2   92%

8. V   S   L   N   No available program appealed to me.
   5   16   13   66%

Figure 1—cont.   QUESTIONNAIRE AND RESULTS

9. V   S   L   N   Didn't want to be apart from my
                              friends.
    1   16   13   66%

10. V   S   L   N   Couldn't afford the personal expenses
                              abroad.
    4   14   20   63%

11. V   S   L   N   Health reasons.
    1   0   4   95%

12. V   S   L   N   Don't like foreign languages.
    1   8   9   81%

13. V   S   L   N   Family didn't want me to go.
    1   1   9   88%

14. V   S   L   N   Missed application deadline.
    1   5   1   93%

15. V   S   L   N   Concern about terrorism or personal
                              safety.
    1   1   7   91%

16. V   S   L   N   Preferred other activity.
    19   11   12   59%

                           Sports: 27%
                           Music: 24%
                           Theater: 12%
                           Art: 3%
                           Resident Advisor: 9%
                           Student Office: 6%
                           Internship/Job   21%

17. V   S   L   N   Preferred U.S. program:
    8   5   1   86%

                           Swarthmore: 21%
                           Colby: 0%
                           Smith: 7%
                           Washington: 14%
                           Transfer: 50%
                           Leave: 7%

18. V   S   L   N   Just wasn't interested.
    5   17   13   65%

19.   Other reasons/comments?

20. If Pomona College had sponsored a summer program
     abroad, would you have considered it?
     YES **58%**   NO **42%**

21. If yes, would you have needed financial aid?
     YES **65%**   NO **35%**

22. Preference (s) for a summer program site:

Australia	8%	Germany/Austria	15%
Canada	3%	Japan	15%
Great Britain	33%	Greece	8%
New Zealand	3%	France, Spain,	
		Scandinavia	5%
Total English-speaking	47%	Latin America, Italy	3%

7

GEORGETOWN UNIVERSITY: THE ARTICULATION OF STUDY ABROAD PROGRAMS AND THE HOME CAMPUS CURRICULUM

William W. Cressey

International programs directors and study abroad advisors have long realized the value of an overseas study experience in the development of intercultural sensitivity, international awareness, and foreign language ability. Now we have reached a stage in the development of international programming activities nationwide when it is appropriate to ask broader questions that relate to a more general student population than the groups with specific international curricular needs and that relate to the entire undergraduate curriculum. Specifically, more and more members of the academic community are recognizing that a study abroad experience can be of value not only to the students of foreign languages, international affairs, international business, and other specifically international fields of study, but also to students in the general liberal arts and sciences and indeed to students in many specialized curricula such as engineering and architecture. As we expand into these new populations, it becomes more and more critical to examine just how the study abroad experience fits into what the student is learning during his/her freshman, sophomore, and senior years. It becomes important to plan carefully for an effective integration of the overseas experience into the home campus curriculum.

Articulation involves at least three stages: planning and assessment by the institution, orientation and preparation of students prior to their departure, and integration of overseas learning experiences into subsequent course work. Although all of these areas have received careful attention at Georgetown University (GU) in the past, the grant from the Ford Foundation to the University of Massachusetts at Amherst provided us with a welcome opportunity to conduct a comprehensive review of our current position and initiate some concrete planning for improvements in these areas. Specifically, the award enabled Georgetown to appoint a faculty seminar group to meet several times during the summer and address specific issues.

PLANNING AND ASSESSMENT

- How adequate are our program review criteria and procedures?
- Are the programs used by Georgetown academically sound?
- Are there programs that are currently being approved that should not be?
- How does the choice of a major relate to the approval of certain programs?
- How should the academic quality of study abroad in developing countries be monitored?
- What enhancements might be included in programs in developing countries in order to evaluate the academic level?
- How successful have we been at encouraging students to attend regular university classes?
- Under what circumstances should we depart from this norm?
- How adequate is the current credit granting procedure?
- Should grades be counted in the QPI (Quality Point Index)?
- Are additional guidelines needed for credit transfer?
- How do courses taken overseas count in the GU curriculum?
- How should they count?
- How do curricular requirements and overseas studies interact?
- What changes are needed if any?

At Georgetown it was recognized that articulation is closely related to evaluation of the academic quality of programs abroad. The International Programs Committee at Georgetown has recently mandated a thorough evaluation project designed to address some of the basic issues on a continuing basis.

From a technical standpoint, the evaluation of quality of overseas programs is accomplished through the credit transfer mechanisms in place in the various Dean's Offices. For this reason the summer faculty seminar group devoted considerable time and energy to issues related to credit transfer. Transfer of credit from overseas study to the Georgetown transcript is accomplished by the dean's office with, in some instances, considerable guidance being provided by academic departments. Questions arose as to the degree of consistency that may or may not exist among schools and departments concerning policy issues related to the transfer of credit. Furthermore, the question arose as to whether transfer of credit is most desirably based on explicit written guidelines, or whether a more impressionistic, human judgment should be the primary determining factor. Most participants in the seminar agreed that both factors are important.

Members of the group interviewed representatives of the deans' offices of the College of Arts and Sciences (CAS), the School of Foreign Service (SFS), the School of Languages and Linguistics (SLL), and the School of Business Administration (SBA). In most instances, the dean decides on general education transfer issues, and in some cases academic departments make decisions on credit to be awarded to satisfy certain majors or concentrations. The two schools that are organized by department (CAS and SLL) make considerable use of the departments, whereas the two schools that are not so organized (SFS and SBA), tend to concentrate the transfer of credit decisions in the Dean's Office.

All agreed that the tradition concerning regulations governing transfer of credit is largely oral, and that deans build up knowledge little by little concerning what seems equivalent to certain Georgetown requirements and what seems appropriate for different groups of students.

The committee felt that greater clarity in the presentation of guidelines, both to students and to faculty, would be desirable. The committee also noted the difficulty in creating such guidelines, pointing out that there is a danger that written guidelines might be so broad as to be meaningless or so specific as to constitute a limiting factor rather than being of real assistance to the academic officers who actually must make the decisions. The committee believed that the effort should be made to construct some guidelines and to publish some materials in the catalogs, either by school or by department.

Questions that might be addressed in such a policy include the following:

(1) What constitutes acceptable courses for the major,

(2) What constitutes acceptable courses for general education requirements, and

(3) What constitutes acceptable programs of study for students in a particular area?

Finally, the listing might state the names of the individuals who have responsibility for making these decisions. In general, the practice seems to be that there is leniency on issues concerning the transferability of courses to satisfy electives or "supporting courses" but a stricter attitude with regard to basic courses.

Another issue that was brought up concerning the transfer of credit had to do with the documentation a student can assemble and bring back to the United States in order to assist the transfer procedures. Students currently receive transcript-like documents from most, if not all, overseas studies programs. In addition. student-written summaries of courses, which might replace the traditional U.S. type syllabi, would be helpful to deans and department representatives trying to make transfer decisions. The example was described of a student who had gone to Oxford and had written such summaries and had his tutors initial them as being fundamentally accurate. The recommendation was that students studying overseas should assemble a sort of academic diary, which would be useful to Georgetown deans and advisors as they evaluate the work done overseas.

QUALITY

The committee discussed issues related to the quality of overseas studies. In one sense, we can distinguish three quality issues: the quality of the host university, the quality of the host program, and the quality of the experience for the Georgetown student.

One important issue particularly, with respect to well respected universities overseas has to do with the different nature of education in Europe and most parts of the world. It was pointed out that the more self-directed, independent nature of European education is indeed one of the values of the overseas experience. Students are expected to behave like adults and may learn to do so partially as a result of this experience. On the other hand, this also entails certain problems in that students may not choose to behave like adults, although they are expected to do so. There was a concern about how Georgetown academic officers can be certain that the experience overseas has been an academically rigorous one, as stated in the current overseas studies guidelines.

A successful model for dealing with the different educational system overseas was found in the Tübingen program. Students meet with German graduate students once a week. These students are designated by the professor and provide supplementary activities; for example, each student writes a weekly essay. The essays are corrected by the graduate students, who also give some direction on readings. Three of the essays are graded by the tutor and the examination at the end is graded by the course professor. The result is two *Scheine*, one for the continuous assessment provided by the tutor, and one for the examination at the end. Other models are possible for other well-recognized universities.

Turning to evaluation of programs, the committee noted that the upfront evaluation is rather thorough. That is to say, a university and potential program is evaluated rather carefully by the Overseas Studies Committee before a GU program is approved.

However, there was some concern that continued evaluation of previously approved Georgetown programs, may not be quite as rigorous. It was recommended that continued evaluation be accomplished in three ways: through the existing area committees, through the creation of some ad hoc committees where the need may arise, and by means of faculty visits. It was pointed out that in addition to providing the means for evaluation, such visits serve to motivate our partners overseas to take the enterprise seriously. The committee also made a strong recommendation that an overseas studies policy statement be adopted by the Council of Deans.

PREPARATION FOR OVERSEAS STUDIES

- How adequate is the current orientation procedure?
- What changes are needed?
- How might more faculty be involved?
- Which currently existing courses might be designated as good preparation for overseas studies?
- Should GU develop a special intercultural communication course similar to those that exist on some campuses?
- What changes if any are needed in the current language requirement for overseas studies

There are several aspects to an appropriate orientation program for students intending to study overseas: logistical and administrative matters and practical information, intercultural communication and related themes, general academic orientation, country specific and university specific information, and content-based information from the academic disciplines.

The group noted that the orientation program as currently organized is quite successful, but it also noted that a number of improvements are possible. Primarily, the current orientation program seems to proceed too quickly and does not span a wide enough range of material. In short, it should be longer and include more. Finally, it was suggested that there should be more faculty involvement in the process, perhaps in the providing of more country-specific material, dealing with political systems, economics, sociology, literature, and so forth.

Three primary possibilities were discussed for ways to improve the orientation program: the creation of a specific course intended for overseas studies participants, the designation of a list of prerequisite courses, at least one of which must be taken by each participant, and third, the extension of the current orientation program by the inclusion of additional meetings and readings. Ultimately, the committee opted to create but not require a specific course and extend the current orientation program.

THE PROPOSED COURSE

The committee discussed existing intercultural courses that are taught on the Georgetown campus (Linguistics Department), have been taught in the past (School of Foreign Service core faculty), and are offered at other universities.
After some discussion, the committee decided to recommend the creation of a course with the following characteristics:
1. The course should have a basic intercultural communication content with some add-on elements by guest lecturers providing country-specific information if this is feasible.

2. The course should be taught using a European teaching style in order to prepare the students for what they are likely to encounter in most parts of the world.

3. A single course should be created, that combines an orientation component with a post-return component. The total credit to be awarded for both components should be three or four credits.

4. In the return part of the course more student participation should be required, for example, a paper that has been started abroad and finished during the fall term of the senior year, reflecting the student's experience abroad and that of others as described during the course, or a discipline based paper (which would have to be graded in most cases by a different member of the faculty). During the second half of the course, a key element would be a seminar approach, during which students would exchange preliminary drafts of their papers for commentary.

Although this course would be limited to overseas studies participants, it is not intended that it be required, and indeed it is not expected that more than about 20% of those studying abroad would have the opportunity to take it.

ENHANCEMENTS OF ORIENTATION

Because the course would be limited to a small percentage of participants in overseas studies programs, it is suggested that several enhancements to the current orientation system be adopted:
1. Two or three lectures given by paid speakers should be incorporated into the orientation program of each student.

These lectures might be country specific or area specific to the extent that this is feasible, given the number of students going to different countries or regions.

2. A portfolio of two or three reading assignments (perhaps articles or essays) should be presented to each student going overseas.

3. An essay based on these reading assignments should be incorporated into the acceptance process.

ENHANCEMENTS UPON THE STUDENTS' RETURN

- How adequate are our reentry procedures?

- What can be done to involve faculty members?

- What enhancements and/or special projects might be added to the overseas experience and related to the senior year?

- Are there specific courses that could make use of the overseas experience in a structured way?

This topic is perhaps the most difficult to deal with and is the one that received the least attention at the Georgetown seminar. Currently students are given a brief reorientation to Georgetown University and an opportunity to discuss their overseas experiences. This is a first step, but much more is probably needed in order to adequately integrate the overseas experience into the four-year continuum of a Georgetown education. Several possible themes were suggested for inclusion in a reorientation post-return session, including:

1. Discussion of what has happened in the United States and at Georgetown during the year abroad.

2. A forum on a theme, at which students will be invited to make presentations. An example discussed somewhat was the "Images of America" concept, with students invited to discuss both the images of the United States that they noted in the country they visited and their own images of the United States, building on the perspectives of an overseas experience.

CONCLUSION

Although much remains to be done, the seminar faculty has made significant progress in defining the issues related to articulation of study abroad programs with the home campus curriculum and has made several concrete suggestions for beginning to address some of these issues. At Georgetown we view the process as a continuous one and intend to embark upon a thorough assessment of individual programs using the concepts designed in this study as guidelines. In this connection we would welcome readers' views on what has been presented here and would be delighted to receive information concerning the experiences of other schools in evaluation and articulation projects.

8

THE UNIVERSITY OF MASSACHUSETTS AT AMHERST: MAKING CONNECTIONS

Maryelise S. Lamet and Carol J. Lebold

International exchange at the University of Massachusetts at Amherst (UM/A) has its roots in the early years of the Massachusetts Agricultural College. In 1876 President William S. Clark traveled to Japan to help establish what became the University of Hokkaido. Having passed its 125th year in 1988, UM/A is the flagship campus of the University of Massachusetts and enjoys a solid reputation as a center of research and teaching excellence.

The student body numbers over 19,000 undergraduate and 6,700 graduate students in nearly 100 fields of study spanning the arts, social sciences, natural sciences, agriculture, education, engineering, health sciences, management, and physical education. The International Programs Office was established in 1969 under the leadership of Barbara B. Burn, associate provost for international programs, to coordinate and develop study abroad and other international activities.

During the 1988-1989 year a total of 383 UM/A students were abroad during the academic year and 289 during summer 1989. In addition, UM/A programs sent 323 non-UM/A students abroad. According to the report on study abroad, enrollments for 1987-1988 published in *Open Doors 1988-89* (published by the Institute of International Education), the University of Massachusetts at Amherst ranked fifth in the nation in the number of students served by its programs.

The geographic scope of current UM/A foreign study programs is broad. Students from over fifty different major fields participated, belying the conventional wisdom that overseas study is for a limited number of majors. Communication majors studied in Denmark, France, Ireland, Israel, Italy, Japan, Spain, and the United Kingdom (UK). School of Management students went to Austria, Canada, Denmark, Egypt, France, Germany,

Ireland, Israel, Japan, Kenya, the People's Republic of China, Spain, and the UK.   Biological Science majors were in Australia, Germany, Ireland, Spain, Sweden, and the UK.

PROJECT IMPLEMENTATION

In order to implement the Study Abroad Articulation Project's (SAAP) goals in spring 1987 a subcommittee of the Committee on Overseas Programs and Exchanges, itself a committee of the Faculty Senate's Foreign and International Studies Council, was appointed with faculty and staff representation. Members of the subcommittee were drawn from the departments of classics, English, French and Italian, history, Spanish and Portuguese, zoology/pre-Med, the Office of Transfer Affairs, and International Programs. Two meetings during the spring of 1987 led to the formulation and initial implementation of the two major lines of inquiry as background for the UM/A SAAP effort to strengthen the relationship between study abroad and the undergraduate curriculum: (1) The articulation of study abroad course work and the student's major course requirements and (2) The articulation of study abroad course work and the recently established UM/A general education requirements.

The priorities chosen by the committee for this project clearly reflect the institution's identity as a large, public university serving the great variety of students in terms of majors and overseas programs available. The emphasis of the project has been on the context for integrating study abroad course work into the student's program of study. While some particular attention was paid to the situation for language majors, the overall focus of the project aimed at enabling all students to articulate or integrate academic work done abroad with what they do in their degree courses in Amherst. The underlying goal was to contribute to the internationalization of undergraduate degree programs.

STUDY ABROAD AND THE MAJOR

The inquiry into policies, practices, and expectations regarding the acceptance of courses done on study abroad to fulfill students' major requirements began with the design of two questionnaires. One was administered to students returned from studying abroad during the 1985-1986 year and fall 1986, and the other to students planning to study abroad during 1987-1988. These instruments focused on the students' motivation, preparation and expectations, particularly as related to course work abroad and their UM/A majors.

The responses to similar questions from both ends of the study abroad experience by these groups and data from other sample student interviews, study abroad evaluation questionnaires and a recent campus-wide international dimensions survey were used to formulate the agenda for this project's implementation. These background data suggested that the following issues are central to the question of how well study abroad course work articulates with major requirements on the home campus:

1.) Timing of the period abroad in the overall undergraduate curriculum.

2.) Availability of information about the details of the curriculum abroad prior to departure from the home campus.

3.) Departmental policies—or the lack of them—regarding the recognition of off-campus course work in meeting major requirements and the department-based junior writing requirement, a one semester course.

4.) Availability of appropriate courses in the major and related fields upon return from study abroad.

During the 1987-1988 academic year, members of the Articulation Project Committee met with faculty from eight departments in the College of Arts and Sciences:

Art	History
Communication	Psychology
Economics	Spanish and Portuguese
French and Italian	Zoology/Pre-Med

The departments targeted for meetings represent a cross-section of the departments in the arts and sciences that already sent significant numbers of students abroad. The inclusion of two language departments allowed the inquiry to contrast and compare language and non-language focused perspectives.

Prior to each departmental meeting, a suggested list of questions was sent to the department. This served as a general guideline for discussions to provide consistency and focus from one meeting to the next. The primary questions discussed at all the one-and-a-half hour departmental meetings were existing policies on off-campus study, faculty goals for study abroad, optimal subjects to be studied abroad, appropriate timing and qualifications for participants in study abroad. The meetings with language department members also addressed the special question of study abroad and the fulfillment of the University of Massachusetts language requirement.

What then did we learn at these departmental meetings? There are definitely certain broad issues that are important to all departments and regarding which there was relative agreement. Specific recommendations were generated from these common concerns. Some differences of opinion on issues such as optimal timing for the study abroad experience reflected the nature of particular departments and policies regarding off-campus study, as well as requirements for specific majors.

Overall, enthusiasm was expressed for students participating in study abroad programs, but there was general agreement that better strategies to disseminate information about the options to students and faculty were crucial. The discussion of timing, departmental policies on major requirements and off-campus study, and the availability of details on courses in specific programs was intertwined with reflections on individual departments' goals for students going abroad.

All departments identified the need to encourage students to consider study abroad as early as possible. Nonetheless, it was clear that there exists a very real contrast between the timing considerations for students who seek to concentrate on courses in the major and those working on language acquisition (for non-language majors) or general education courses.

Several departments, notably History and Economics, have sufficiently flexible requirements so that study abroad may be inserted with relatively little difficulty at virtually any point in the student's academic career. Some concern was expressed in these departments that students in non-English speaking countries pursue adequately advanced courses in their major while continuing language study. In general, the more electives in the major requirements of a department, the greater the flexibility in all these areas.

Students majoring in fields in which course sequencing is important experience greater difficulty in timing their study abroad—if they can do it at all. The Zoology and Art departments present interesting contrasts on this dilemma. In the Zoology Department, students must fulfill very specific requirement during the first two years, which provide the building blocks for the major. Study abroad in the junior and senior year is actually made easier by this fact—particularly in light of the universality of the teaching of the natural sciences.

By contrast, studio art majors also need basic building block work in the Foundation Program (first year in the major) and a semester or two following it, but they must also produce a Bachelor of Fine Arts (BFA) project involving a portfolio and show. This makes the choice of time for study abroad more delicate in light of the need for close work with on-campus faculty for the BFA project.

Another interesting contrast emerges in the area of whether students should seek course work abroad that primarily replicates the home-campus curriculum, which is the attitude of the Zoology Department faculty and which is likely to be shared by most faculty in the natural and applied sciences, or take courses that may not be represented in the UM/A course catalog, which is the view of the Art and Communication department faculty, who seek to have more of the basics pursued at home. This contrast represents the same tension within the major field, that exists in regard to the whole undergraduate curriculum of whether study abroad course work should be primarily mainline courses that are integrated or primarily enrichment courses (language, culture, etc.) that are grafted on. While to some extent the position of a department on this question is a reflection of the amount of perceived "free space" in the major's curriculum for non-prescribed work, it is also centrally related to a department faculty's willingness to grant credit towards students' requirements for their major courses taken abroad. Some change is now taking place in the United States in this area.

The size and nature of student demand for a major has bearing on the articulation process. Majors such as economics, psychology, and communication have requirements that students must fulfill before being fully accepted as majors. The large group of pre-majors in these fields presents a very real challenge in advising students on what to take while abroad because they may not be fully accepted in the major when they must begin to apply for and choose among program options. In some cases this means that students are advised to take courses for general education requirements or to fill elective space.

Language study introduces other important issues into the discussion. Interestingly, the language departments participating in our meetings both recommend that students go abroad as early as the sophomore year, having taken language courses for several semesters in their first year. Reasons for this are numerous. The departments point out that immersion produces superior students, both among language and non-language majors. Going abroad early allows the majors to return and further develop their skills with a stronger base, while non-majors frequently use study abroad as the doorway into a minor or double major in the study abroad country's language. This spin-off is of particular interest to a department like Spanish and Portuguese at UM/A, which serves over 3,000 students of mixed motivation outside the major pursuing language requirements. In refreshing contrast, students returning from study abroad are highly motivated and interested in upper-level courses, which they often integrate into a wide variety of majors in a true sense of articulation.

The diversity of possible approaches to articulation already mentioned were brought up by the faculty members with whom we met, and reflect the fact that study abroad can be integrated with the home campus curriculum, but careful attention must be paid to the needs of each student early in the advising process—both by International Programs staff and departmental advisors. While the articulation of courses taken abroad into the major presents a challenge to departments, all faculty members expressed a delight in teaching and working with the study abroad returnees. Most believed that the challenges and experiences of study abroad—

academic and personal—produce highly motivated, actively involved students.

All departments stressed the need to find more creative and far-ranging ways to reach students in their field.   Faculty members were often motivated by the meetings to ask new questions regarding programs of particular interest to their students and to see more clearly the merits of close collaboration with the International Programs Office on a variety of efforts. Thus, the meetings proved provocative both in raising the question of articulation and reasserting the importance of study abroad as an option for more students.

STUDY ABROAD AND GENERAL EDUCATION

Since the University of Massachusetts at Amherst's general education requirements recently came into effect, students going abroad after January 1988 were the first major groups to be affected. For the past decade many U.S. institutions of higher education have been reevaluating the makeup of the core curriculum in a liberal arts education. At UM/A this process has been guided by the General Education Council of the Faculty Senate and has led to new requirements that expose the student to the "social world" (arts, historical studies, and social and behavioral sciences), the "biological and physical world," and "analytical reasoning" (mathematics and logic).   The articulation committee worked with members of the General Education Council in several areas as the new regulations came into effect.

The recognition of study abroad course work in fulfilling overall general education requirements. The Study Abroad Articulation Project provided an important impetus to International Programs and the Office of Transfer Affairs to discuss both the substance of study abroad course work relevant to the general education requirements and the mechanisms necessary for the recognition of the completion overseas of a requirement to take place.   An advising sheet "Guidelines for Students wishing to take courses for General Education Credit While on International Exchange", was jointly drawn up. This sheet has been made part of the standard information given to all students accepted to study abroad. In the early stages of the new requirements, it seeks to provide general guidelines for students to follow in choosing courses for which they will request general education credit. Strong communication between International Programs and the Office of Transfer Affairs and careful advising of students have been crucial in helping students to make the right connections.

On the practical level, the discussions between International Programs and the office of Transfer Affairs also led to reformatting the forms used for preliminary approval and transfer of international credit. The new forms, currently being used, will be refined as necessary to assist in keeping track of both general education and major credit designations for courses completed during study abroad. As UM/A moves into a system to allow degree auditing, the work carried out for the SAAP will continue to help the student going abroad with the important mechanics of integration of the courses taken abroad into his/her degree requirement structure. In time, computerized record keeping of overseas courses will allow students to check which courses have received general education or major recognition. While this will be helpful, the UM/A emphasis upon direct enrollment in overseas institutions will always mean that the range of possible courses to be taken abroad will be as wide as the curricula of those institutions themselves. Thus, the importance of good communication and collaboration between International Programs and the Office of Transfer Affairs will remain central.

The recognition of study abroad course work in fulfilling part of the general education social and cultural diversity component, a two-course requirement within the social world requirement. The Study Abroad Articulation Project Subcommittee brought the following proposal to the University's General Education Council: "One of the social and cultural diversity component designations may be fulfilled if a student takes a course during a semester or academic year abroad within the realm of the social world."

The committee's rationale was that while the social and cultural diversity component specifies that "Courses satisfying this requirement shall reach beyond the perspectives of mainstream American culture and Western tradition," our proposal suggests that, whether in the non-Western world or in the Western world, the study abroad immersion experience that involves a substantial period of time (semester or academic year) fulfills directly the explicit goals of the component. Surveys carried out by International Programs at the University of Massachusetts and by others involved with international interchange strongly support the assumption that studying for a significant period in another culture leads to a pluralistic outlook. In other words, study abroad, whether in the Western or non-Western world, gives students critical knowledge and insights on cultural diversity and on many relevant aspects of ethnocentric stereotypes.

This proposal was discussed in a number of meetings of the General Education Council and the Faculty Senate. It had not yet been adopted in early 1990, but the the Study Abroad Articulation Project Committee and the International Programs Office will continue to address this issue. It is hoped that as the interpretation of general education requirements evolves, the above proposal may be accepted.

RECOMMENDATIONS

The final meeting of the project phase of the UM/A Study Abroad Articulation Sub-committee took place in mid-May 1988. The group discussed the results of the student surveys and the minutes of the eight departmental meetings. In addition, the activity of the committee during spring 1988 relating to the issue of recognizing that courses taken abroad can fulfill the new General Education requirements was a major focus of discussion. The major recommendations of the committee were:

1. The Study Abroad Articulation Committee should continue to meet as a subcommittee of the Committee on Overseas Programs and Exchanges of the Faculty Senate.

2. The polling of student opinion on issues related to the articulation of study abroad and home-campus curriculum should continue.

3. Regarding meetings with departments' faculty on the model developed during 1987-1988, the contacts and understanding gained through these meetings provide International Programs with significant insights that, while to some extent generalizable, should also continue to be pursued on a department-specific basis. The focus should be broadened to include departments in the professional faculties.

4. A number of specific recommendations should be presented to appropriate deans, departments, and committees.

   • Introduction of entries on study abroad opportunities into department sections of the university catalog and department handbooks.

   • Organization of more department-specific meetings on study abroad opportunities, using returned study abroad participants who are majors as a resource. Development as desired of department-specific information sheets on program options.

   • Clarification of policy and dissemination of information on the opportunities presented by study abroad for completion of the language requirement. This effort will require discussion with the language department faculty not yet surveyed and raises the prospect of expanded developments in the area of sophomore year study abroad.

   • Continuation of work with the General Education Council to develop the most effective policies possible on the application of study abroad course work to the general education requirements.

- Orientation sessions to be offered to students going on non-UM/A programs.

International Programs staff will work with the SAAP Committee to implement the above proposals.

5. The work of the SAAP needs to be brought to broader campus attention.

FOLLOW-UP

During fall 1988 a number of the recommendations bore fruit. The Study Abroad Articulation Project Committee met and directed International Programs staff to work on the recommendations that (1) departments be encouraged to include reference to study abroad in their catalog entries and (2) department-based study abroad information meetings be held. Various models of department-based study abroad information meetings were held with the cooperation of faculty in the History, Hotel, Travel and Restaurant Administration, and Psychology departments. This practice will be continued and expanded in upcoming semesters.

The *1989-90 UM/A Catalog* will include new references to study abroad in the entries of the following departments: Art, Communication, Economics, English, History, Psychology, Spanish and Portuguese, and Zoology/Pre-Med. These entries focus on study abroad as a positive element in a student's undergraduate career, thus highlighting in a very important university document the positive connection between study abroad and the home campus curriculum.

CONCLUSION

At the University of Massachusetts at Amherst the Study Abroad Articulation Project encouraged inquiry into extremely significant issues related to international education and the UM/A curriculum. This resulted in strong support by the Study Abroad Articulation Subcommittee for the basic premise that study abroad can and does play an important role in internationalizing the undergraduate curriculum. Furthermore, it has generated concrete recommendations of how faculty and students can be made more aware of the significant academic goals that can be fulfilled during the study abroad period.

The collaboration between the Office of Transfer Affairs and the International Programs Office to continue evaluating student goals and expectations related to study abroad and their curriculum is an important new overture. The work with departments undertaken as part of this project has raised timely questions and suggests that focusing on recruitment at the departmental level is very important. Close contacts between International Programs and faculty involved in departmental advising will strengthen the articulation of study abroad course work and the home-campus curriculum.

It is believed that the continued activities of the Study Abroad Articulation Subcommittee will significantly assist in integrating study abroad more fully into the undergraduate curriculum of the University of Massachusetts at Amherst, thereby bringing a greater internationalization of this curriculum. It is hoped that the UM/A experience may suggest useful approaches for study abroad professionals and faculty at other institutions as well.

9

SMITH COLLEGE: IMPACTS ON THE HOME-CAMPUS AND INTERNATIONAL STUDIES CURRICULUM OF SMITH'S STRONG STUDY ABROAD COMMITMENT

Robert C. Davis and Patricia C. Olmstead

Early in 1987 the Ford Foundation awarded $50,000, which was divided among eight institutions to support projects or studies on how to foster articulation between study abroad programs and home campus liberal arts curricula. Smith College's participation in that project took place over an eighteen-month period from January 1, 1987 through June 30, 1988. The chief objective of the proposed project was to examine problems in and impediments to the articulation between American students' study abroad experience and curricular programs in the liberal arts at their home institutions and to develop strategies and policies that enhance this articulation. The long-range goal will be to enable study abroad programs to be more a part of and feed into efforts to strengthen undergraduate international studies at U.S. colleges and universities.

Smith College was a natural choice for participation in such a project because of its long and extensive history in the concept and implementation of the "junior year abroad" and other study abroad experiments. Immediately following the University of Delaware's establishment in 1923 of the first junior year abroad program in France, the then President of Smith, William Allan Neilson, determined that Smith would be the first women's college to set up its own program abroad.

The "experiment" in Paris was instituted for the 1925-1926 academic year and continues to this day, having experienced only a brief suspension during the World War II period. The additional history of the "junior years abroad" is outlined here, reflecting Smith's pursuits not only over a sixty-year period in Western Europe but, as long as fifty years ago, in Central and other North American countries and, more recently, in the Pacific Rim area.

CALENDAR OF JUNIOR YEAR ABROAD PROGRAMS

1925   First junior year abroad program established in France
1930   Junior year abroad program established in Spain
1931   Junior year abroad program established in Italy
1931   Plans for junior year abroad in Germany approved, to be
        established when and if possible
1936   Program in Spain suspended
1937   Junior year abroad in Mexico established (one year only)
1939   Programs in France and Italy suspended
1944   Program in Mexico resumed (1944-1952)
1945   Exchange program established with the University of
        Toronto (1945-1972)
1946   Junior year abroad program established in Switzerland
        (1946-present)
1947   Programs in France and Italy resumed (1947-present)
1947   Program in Spain resumed (1947-1971)
1961   Program established in Germany (1961-present)
1966   Junior year abroad program established in the Philippines
        (1966-1972)
1967   Exchange program established with the University of
        Sussex (1967-1986)
1968   Exchange program established with the University of
        Leicester (1968-present)

By the end of the 1987-1988 academic year, over 5,000 students
(Smith and non-Smith) will have participated in these programs.

Although the earlier programs were set up as language and
literature programs by the relevant Smith foreign language
departments, later programs such as those in Geneva and in the
Philippines emphasized international studies, law, politics,
and/or economics. It was the difference between these two types of
programs—the language-based program and the international
studies-based program—that had raised some questions internally
at Smith about the continuing attractiveness of the former
(language-based) programs in contrast to the less enduring and
diminishing latter (international studies-based) programs that we
had hoped to address as a segment of the present inquiry. The
programs in Florence, Hamburg, and Paris continue to flourish,
but over the past years concern has been growing on the Smith
campus over the apparent lack of faculty interest in study abroad
for students who, at the same time, are becoming increasingly
exposed to and involved in international affairs and global issues.

Meetings of appropriate committees and departments involved
in international studies have repeatedly proven discouraging and
unfruitful. Many faculty members teaching in traditional
international studies programs have had relatively little
"international" experience or exposure themselves and do not see
study abroad options as particularly desirable components in
their fields. And only a modest number of those faculty members

are fluent in a language other than English. Over the past 5 to 10-year period, students have often reported that several advisors in those international studies departments (politics, economics, sociology, philosophy) have been openly discouraging in advising potential study abroad students for Smith's own as well as other junior year abroad programs.

At the same time, however, the college has expanded its curricular offerings to include area or interdepartmental studies such as: latin American studies major (1986), Jewish studies minor (1986), Third World development studies minor (1986), Certificate of African studies (1987), and East Asian studies major (1988). With the implementation of these new programs, majors, and minors has come a growing student interest in study abroad and an expansion of the geographic areas open to study abroad.

Approximately seventy-five Smith students participate annually in Smith's own four junior year abroad programs. In addition, the college has consortial affiliations with other sponsoring institutions: classics (Intercollegiate Center for Classical Studies, Rome), Japanese (Associated Kyoto Program), Spanish (Programa de Estudios Hispanios en Cordoba), and sociology (University of Leicester, England). Without formal affiliation but with the college's approval of study abroad programs run by other colleges or institutions, forty to fifty Smith students study abroad annually at institutions around the world, 95% of them participating in full-year programs (Table 1).

Table 1.
SUMMARY OF JUNIORS STUDYING ABROAD 1983-1988

Class of Away	1985	1986	1987	1988	1989
Academic year	1983-84	1984-85	1985-86	1986-87	1987-88
On Smith junior year abroad Programs					
Florence	8	3	8	13	13
Geneva	17	22	21	16	10
Hamburg	10	10	7	11	18
Paris	33	40	39	36	33
Total Smith JYA Participants	68	75	75	76	74
On other programs abroad					
Kyoto	1	2	2	1	4
ICCS, Rome	1	5	1	2	-
Cordoba, Spain	3	7	7	11	2
United Kingdom	46	40	25	37	45

Class of	1985	1986	1987	1988	1989
Away					
Academic year	1983-84	1984-85	1985-86	1986-87	1987-88
Western Europe	12	8	6	5	8
Middle East	3	1	2	-	4
Other	5	6	5	16	16
Total other programs abroad	71	69	48	72	79
Total Abroad	139	144	123	148	153
Percentage of class abroad	21	22	20	23	24
Total number of junior class, as of September	664	664	624	644	647

Structure/Administration of Study Abroad

Nevertheless, in spite of a long and well-recognized history in study abroad, and, in spite of the addition of new majors and minors with international components and obvious international emphasis, it is not clear that on the Smith campus either faculty, departments, or the administration has been deeply committed to the internationalization of the campus or to increasing students' awareness of or participation in international study, research, work, or activities. Except for pertinent language faculty there appears to be very little overall faculty understanding or support for study abroad as a regular curricular option, and perhaps less than a third of the faculty of 270 members are knowledgeable even about Smith's own programs.

For the administration of the college's own programs and for the screening and dissemination of study abroad opportunities in general, the college's Committee on Study Abroad, a standing faculty committee, is appointed annually to serve those functions. The Committee consists of the dean of the college (chair), the associate dean for intercollegiate study, the treasurer, one faculty representative from each of the Smith College junior year abroad programs (normally a former director) and five other appointed faculty members with divisional representation. Its purpose and mandate is to review all concerns of the Smith junior year abroad programs, consider policy matters related to the programs, review nominations and recommend to the president directors for the Smith programs, meet with student representatives returned from study abroad programs, oversee publicity and information material for the Smith programs, select students for participation, and review and monitor Smith students' requests for transfer credit for other non-Smith programs.

The full committee meets at least three times a year to discuss issues of policy, exceptions to established procedures, or to consider new recommendations concerning study abroad. Most of the committee's work is done through subcommittees that meet much more frequently and deal with ongoing issues and immediate requests. The subcommittees process about 300 applications per year.

Because the range of expertise and interests of members on the committee varies so enormously, years alternate from intensively productive ones to years when the absence of crises prompts very little activity; ongoing, long-term issues become somewhat obscured or remain for the time being unaddressed.

During the 1987-1988 academic year the committee was heartened to hear from an ad hoc group of eleven faculty members requesting Smith's increased investigations into opportunities for and involvement in providing study abroad options in Third World countries. Those eleven faculty members represented a range of disciplines: Afro-American studies, anthropology, geology, history, Latin American studies, mathematics, religion, Spanish, and Portuguese.

Their concerns ranged from the rather basic requests that more information on Third World programs be made available and publicized for students as visibly as Smith's Western Europe programs are publicized, to finding ways to remove the financial aid barriers for students who might wish to participate in Third World study abroad programs. Two members of that ad hoc group will join the committee for the next academic year.

The college always has a core of twenty-five to thirty faculty members who have previously served as directors of Smith or other study abroad programs and an additional twenty faculty who have served as exchange faculty at foreign universities. Smith has ongoing faculty exchanges with the University of Hamburg, where one of the Smith programs is located, as well as exchanges previously with the Universities of Sussex, Leicester, and Florence.

Several years ago it was determined that each academic department would appoint one of its members as the study abroad advisor for majors in that department, and they work with varying resources and success. Information is provided to them through the Committee on Study Abroad as well as from their own departmental colleagues, and students are referred to them initially from listings in the college catalog.

Pre- and Post-language Study

Our investigation at Smith College had originally been intended to focus on the impact of study abroad on pre- and post-language study, with the expectation of discovering whether emphasis on preparing for study abroad and upon students returning from abroad deterred other potential language majors or non-language majors from continued language study at the advanced level, and whether any determination could be made to show an effect, positive or negative, on the development of an international studies curriculum at the college.

In fall 1987 a committee was formed (in part from an ad hoc committee simultaneously engaged in a departmental self-study on the multiple curricular and staffing needs and complexities of the various language departments), which polled the nine language departments via a modest questionnaire (Figure 1). Although the questionnaire was distributed also to three social science departments whose curricula comprise much of international studies and each of which sends a significant number of majors abroad, the committee decided that their responses, or lack of responses, would not be useful for the project. However, from the nine language departments' responses we are able to report somewhat differing but real pedagogical curricular offerings, needs, successes, and failures. The long history of Smith in study abroad programs has necessitated and nurtured strong foreign language teaching at the college and high expectations on the part of students and the foreign host universities for quality preparation in the languages, literatures, and cultures of the host countries.

The foreign language departments must also provide a curriculum that addresses not only the needs of students planning to go or returning from abroad, but as preparation for graduate study, for the increasing number of "area studies" offerings and academic minors recently adopted into the Smith curriculum and, hopefully, toward increased post-college involvement in global literacy and concerns.

Responses to the questionnaire by the Foreign Language departments can be summarized as follows:

Question 1 - *Are any introductory courses in your department geared particularly toward prospective study abroad participants?*

German and Italian specifically cited their intensive or accelerated course, while the Chinese and Japanese elementary courses offered are automatically intensive courses. The Russian and French departments believed that all their introductory offerings applied, whereas in Spanish and Portuguese none of the courses is specifically geared toward study abroad.

Question 2 - *What curricular changes have been made or new courses developed largely to prepare students for study abroad?*

Both Chinese and Japanese instructors cited the change from a "standard" elementary tract to an intensive format for all beginning courses as a move designed largely to insure the better preparation of their students for study abroad. Russian and Spanish and Portuguese instructors emphasized the integration and updating of contemporary cultural materials in courses for the beginning, intermediate, and advanced levels. French Department faculty members referred to the reintroduction of the "newspapers" course and Italian instructors noted the strengthening of the survey of literature course in preparation for student work in Florence, while the German Department has increased the conversational and "everyday" cultural components of both the fourth semester language courses and the conversation and composition offering.

The Italian, Japanese, Russian, and Spanish and Portuguese departments cite no specific new courses. The Chinese and French faculty both developed newspaper courses in their respective departments to facilitate students' familiarization with the respective foreign culture. German instructors designed a civilization course specifically to give students preparing to go abroad both the general background they might need as well as experience with the primarily lecture format of many German university courses.

Question III - *What curricular changes have been made or new courses developed largely for majors and minors who do not participate in study abroad?*

The French, Italian, Japanese, and Spanish and Portuguese departments report no courses largely for those juniors remaining on campus. The Russian department cites flexibility in the civilization major, which allows students on campus a broad range of options, with Chinese listing the newspaper Chinese course as also sharing in this role. The German faculty developed an upper-level intermediate culture and writing course designed to assist those students who do not study abroad with developing some of the language and culture skills the others learn abroad. In addition, the German Department dropped the number of courses required for the major from ten to nine (above the basis of at least four semesters in the language) to ensure that students who did not study abroad could still readily complete the major.

Question 4 A - *If courses have been specifically designed for study abroad participants, can you give details on how the design differs from the usual course at that level?*

The Japanese, Italian, and Spanish and Portuguese departments offered no response to this question. The Russian Department cited new cultural materials and an emphasis on oral proficiency training as the major distinction. The French faculty noted the difference in content between the civilization course on the French press and other offerings, where the focus was on contemporary articles "as is" on politics, the arts, society in

general, daily life, and so on rather than literature and history.
The Chinese faculty echoed the French distinction for the
newspaper Chinese course but added the significance of the course
for the understanding of journalistic jargon as well as political
and technical terminology.   Lastly, the German accelerated
language course differs from the standard beginning track by
offering daily meetings and emphasizing active practice in the
language with more attention given to the cultural context.

Question 4 B - *When were they instituted into the curriculum?
Dropped? Why?*

New materials for the Russian courses were introduced five
years ago and have been steadily updated. The French newspapers
course was instituted six years ago but due to staffing restrictions,
it has only been offered occasionally. The department plans to
reintroduce it in fall 1988. The German Department introduced
an experimental beginning course for students with some high
school German but not enough preparation for the intermediate
level. Previously they had usually been placed in the accelerated
course, which often caused problems for them as well as those
with no previous German but the desire to prepare themselves for
study abroad. Staffing restrictions forced the cancellation of this
course after only one year in 1986-1987.

Question 5 - *How do senior courses attempt to integrate the
study abroad experience into the curriculum?*

Chinese faculty did not respond to this question, while the
Russian instructors reiterated the problem of staffing restrictions
as the reason why the department can offer little more than the
standard advanced courses. Senior seminars in Italian are offered
on an alternating basis and are coordinated with the courses
taken in Florence, whereas the Spanish and Portuguese
Department stresses the integration of a great variety of cultural
experience not just from returnees but from Hispanic students as
well.   The Japanese faculty introduced 300-level courses three
years ago to a large extent in order to accommodate the junior
year returnees and allow them and other students of advanced
language proficiency to continue their Japanese language studies.
To a large degree, the French Department bases its expectations on
and adjusts the level of its advanced courses to the linguistic and
cultural sophistication of the students returning from Paris and
Geneva.   The French faculty noted the multiple benefits of the
junior year abroad experience for the department in that the
returnees not only allow for the advanced level of the upper
division courses but provide motivation for the students in the
lower division classes as well. Finally, all senior German majors
are required to take an advanced translation and style course and
the senior seminar. The style course serves largely to bring the
writing ability of the returnees up to the level of their other
linguistic skills. By introducing a similar course on the upper-
intermediate level, the department was able to keep the advanced

course on the post-Hamburg level, while simultaneously preparing those students who do not go abroad. The senior seminar affords all majors the opportunity to participate in a seminar environment similar to that of a German university.

Question 6 - *What courses have been introduced into the department's curriculum to tie in with the introduction of international relations courses?*

Only the Russian Department responded to this question by making a general reference to the Russian civilization major.

Question 7 - *What percentage of your department do you estimate supports the study abroad experience as an integral component of the major?*

100% enthusiastically: French, German, Italian, Japanese, and Russian

90% enthusiastically: Spanish and Portuguese

10% moderately: Spanish and Portuguese

No response: Chinese

From these responses, we moved to examine in more detail the curricular changes instituted over the past five years by our own German Department, which runs one of the college's year-long programs in Hamburg, and by our Japanese Department, which does not have its own program abroad but is affiliated with the Associated Kyoto Program (AKP), and, in addition, sends students on other colleges' programs in Japan. These case studies exemplify some of the problems, limitations, and possible solutions to many problems of articulation between study abroad and the curriculum.

German Case Study - GER 110d "Accelerated Elementary German" has long been the beginning course that has produced the most candidates for study abroad in Hamburg. We encourage new students to German who might want to participate in the junior year program to complete this course, which covers the material of three semesters in two so that they might take as much German as possible by the end of their sophomore year. GER 110d differs from the standard elementary track (GER 100) primarily in intensity, meeting five days a week for two more hours per week while covering the course work found in both GER 100 and the intermediate second year course, GER 120. Since students meet daily, they have a greater opportunity to progress steadily, especially in spoken German. Hence oral skills are emphasized, with more attention given to the cultural context. Furthermore, students in GER 110d are expected to be more highly motivated to learn and are therefore given more of the responsibility of learning the grammar at home so that more class time is devoted to active practice in the foreign language.

In 1986-1987, GER 115 "Advanced Elementary German" was introduced so that those first-year students with German experience from high school who placed between GER 100 and GER 120 would not be forced into GER 110d if they did not want to participate in an intensive course. GER 110d could then better fulfill its purpose as described above, while students with previous German who were not preparing for study abroad could continue in a course designed to meet their special needs. Unfortunately, staffing considerations have led to its bracketing.

During the past two years, GER 130 "Intermediate German II" and GER 221 "Reading, Conversation and Composition" have been modified to meet better the needs of students preparing to go abroad. The emphasis in the former course lies with developing reading skills, progressing to extended, unedited literary and journalistic texts, while the conversational components of GER 221 have been strengthened with special attention to conversational strategies and idiomatic expression. Weekly assignments also allow the study abroad candidate to gain practice in various forms of writing, such as business and personal letters, vitae, diary, and essay.

In 1985-1986, GER 281 "German Civilization" was developed to a large extent to help prepare students for the typically specialized courses abroad by providing them with a course in which the history and interrelationships of such specific events and figures are traced. While still a course primarily in German culture, the nature of its material lends itself well to inclusion in that list of courses supporting the International Studies Program. In its form as well, GER 281 with its lecture format serves to prepare students for a typical European course structure seldom practiced in American departments of foreign language and literature.

GER 240 "Analyzing and Writing Contemporary German," first offered in 1986-1987, was designed primarily for students who do not choose to participate in the Hamburg program but desire an upper-200-level language course. Through the use of film, videotapes, taped interviews, and song lyrics, as well as print materials, including advertisements, newspaper articles, letters, cartoons, speeches, official forms, and literary selections, GER 240 attempts to bring the cultural context closer to the student remaining on the home campus. By practicing "proficiency in context," the student learns to master many of the discourse strategies commonly experienced during the Hamburg year. Of course, Hamburg candidates may also take the course, provided they have fulfilled the prerequisites, and staffing restrictions have, in fact, led to mixing both groups in the course.

All senior German majors are required to take GER 340 "Advanced Studies in Translation and Style" and GER 351 "Senior Seminar." GER 340 serves largely to bring the returning Hamburg students' writing ability up to the level of their other language skills (reading, speaking, comprehension), which generally improve abroad at a much faster rate than writing. The creation of GER 240 allows the department to keep the level of GER 340 at the post-Hamburg level, while bringing along those German students who remained at home. GER 351 affords all advanced students the opportunity of participating in a seminar environment similar to that at a German university and to write an extended analysis in German. We attempt not only to match the level and content of a European seminar but, perhaps more importantly, allow the student to continue the kind of independent work the study abroad experience fosters. Our returnees often feel stifled by the constraints of many courses on campus—with reading lists and assigned weekly quizzes and papers—after having learned to identify, define, and conduct research on a topic on their own during the junior year abroad.

Lastly, the number of courses required for the German major has been reduced from ten to nine above the basis in part to insure that students who do not go to Hamburg can still complete the major even if their first two year's work was spent completing the basis requirements (GER 100a and b, 120a, 130b). While one of our departmental goals remains preparing students for study in Germany, we believe that several of the changes listed above, along with the introduction of the German minor in 1985-1986, have encouraged and enabled students interested in German but not in study abroad to complete their studies on campus. We have seen no data that would indicate that an emphasis on preparation for study abroad has deterred students from continuing their work in German at Smith.

Japanese Case Study - The first Smith study abroad student was sent to Japan in 1974, just two years after the Japanese language and literature programs began at the college in 1972.

Japanese language courses had originally been offered at the first- and second-year levels three hours a week like many standard track Western language courses at Smith. It was soon evident, however, that this time allotment was not sufficient for an American student to acquire even basic skills in Japanese because of its linguistic difference from Indo-European languages as well as dissimilarities in the cultural background that impede the learning of the language.

As an initial step toward overcoming these problems, the first-year language course was changed to an intensive format in the academic year 1985-1986, increasing the instruction time to five hours a week and requiring a year-long enrollment for twelve credits. For the second year, one fifty-minute class was added unofficially to the regular three seventy-minute sessions and year-long enrollment was required, without an increase in credit. Though the first year course is called intensive, it still differs from intensive Japanese courses offered at many other universities and colleges in the following ways:

1.) Intensive courses normally meet for eight fifty-minute classes, three of which are taught by the main instructor and five discussion or drill classes conducted by teaching assistants.

2.) Such courses normally count as two courses (i.e. the credits received are double that of a standard semester course).

3.) Second-year Japanese courses are also intensive in these programs.

From these differences it becomes clear that a Smith student who studied two years of Japanese (particularly before 1986) and went to Japan during her junior year would have a handicap, at least at the time of the placement test for the program in Japan. For this reason, as well as because of the anticipated increase in the enrollment in Japanese courses as requirements for the newly established East Asian studies interdepartmental major, it is urgent that the language courses—especially the second-year course—be further restructured. This need is also felt among other Japanese programs in the Five Colleges as well as by the Center for East Asian Studies (CEAS), which is encouraging each institution to develop intensive courses in East Asian languages as well as establishing advanced courses in the field.

Because of the increasing number of requests made by students continuing language instruction beyond the 200 (second-year) level, and also in order to accommodate the returnees from study abroad programs, Five Colleges Inc. created a new teaching position in 1985 with the intention of beginning 300-level courses, and Smith College has been hosting this position during the 1987-1988 academic year. This advanced Japanese language course has been offered at Smith for three years for students from Smith, Amherst, and Mount Holyoke Colleges, all of which are AKP members yet never had upper-level courses in Japanese.

In the first semester it was offered at Smith (fall 1985), this course had three post-200 Smith students and five students who varied in their background of study and/or experience living in Japan. The difference in the levels between the two groups was striking: post-200 Smith students were at a clear disadvantage because of the lack of intensity in their previous training, particularly in their oral-communicative skills. The instructor found it very difficult to adjust for the discrepancy between the two groups. Moreover, some students who returned from AKP that year had to take individual special studies because they were even more advanced than those in the 300 course, and they also felt it a step backward to join the post-200 students after their extra year of intensive Japanese abroad.

The same problem continued the next year, 1986-1987, so we offered a 350 course in the spring semester in order to accommodate those returning from their junior year in Japan and reserved the existing 300 course for the post-200 students. We were able to offer this extra language course only by dropping a literature course that year. Meanwhile, during the same year, 1986-1987, we made great efforts to improve and upgrade the first two years' instruction, giving much consideration to all of the problems mentioned above. Proficiency-oriented instruction was adopted in order to develop the students' communicative competence, a variety of audiovisual materials were utilized, and extensive reading materials were used for comprehension and discussion in Japanese. This effort was enhanced by the coordination of teaching materials among the Five College Japanese programs, with all programs adopting the same, recently published textbook.

In 1987 we realized the first success of our efforts when we found that the second-year students started out the course with much enhanced oral skills and a clearer understanding of the social aspects of the language. The post-200 students who continued on to the 300-level course, moreover, were competitive with the returnees who had taken Japanese 200 during 1985-1986.

This progress, however, implies another future problem: the students who go to study abroad now will again likely be far more advanced when they return than the future post-200 students because of their better preparation and probable faster progress in Japanese during their year in Japan; as a result, they will not be accommodated by the 300-level courses. Thus, while we have significantly improved the first two years of language training so that present post-200 Smith students are at a similar level as those returning from Japan (who have not had the benefits of the new program), in the near future we will once again have to face the problem of a need for more advanced course(s) as these same students begin to return from an intensive second year of Japanese language training in Japan.

Based on these facts, the following is a summary of the problems awaiting future resolution:

1.) A need to make second-year Japanese intensive, with an appropriate credit increase. This will become urgent (a) because of the rapid increase in both enrollment and interest in Japanese at Smith College among students in various fields (economics, art, international relations, etc.), as well as East Asian studies majors and (b) in order to match and maintain the quality of the intensive language courses at the national level.

2.) A need to develop 300-level and/or more advanced-level courses. Every year the number of students who are interested in study abroad is increasing, and we are in the process of expanding affiliated programs other than AKP (because AKP itself has become overextended), such as exchange programs with Doshisha Women's College and Japan Women's University. Within the next three to four years, the number of study abroad students is anticipated to double or triple the current number, and we must seriously concern ourselves with how to accommodate their requests for continuing the study of Japanese after their return to campus, without aggravating the current situation in the 300-level courses.

The above summary concerns only the language courses in our program. We must, of course, continue to offer literature courses, and we will need to offer more courses in literature in the future to develop the program and ensure the integrity of the major program. However, with the size of the current faculty (two full-time positions) such tasks appear to be very difficult to complete.

In addition to our questionnaire and case studies, we have begun to collect data on pre- and post-study abroad students, tracking their post-abroad studies, the variation of their course choices with those of language majors who have not studied abroad, and the academic performances of both groups.

CONCLUSIONS AND RECOMMENDATIONS

Our first conclusion is that only those foreign language departments that are specifically associated with or sponsor a Smith junior year program wholeheartedly support study abroad and specifically design language courses toward that end. We conclude also that outside of our foreign language departments there is only passive interest or knowledge among our faculty of the study abroad opportunities available to or appropriate for their student majors. Finally, there is little apparent effort on campus to integrate study abroad into our international relations curriculum or its contributory departments.

The Study Abroad Articulation Project, then, has given us the impetus to undertake the following steps over the next two-year period:

1. Poll our entire faculty on their foreign language and international back-grounds: fluency, residence abroad, schooling abroad, attitudes toward undergraduate study abroad, interests in special study abroad opportunities such as summer programs, tours, and so forth.

2. Design and distribute a more informative pre-departure questionnaire addressing language preparation, cultural expectations, knowledge of social, political, and economic history of the host country; knowledge of social, political, cultural, and economic history of the United States.

3. Design and distribute a questionnaire for students returning from abroad, addressing questions similar to those above as well as academic expectations or choices subsequent to the study abroad experience.

4. Through our standing faculty committee attempt to reach a larger portion of the faculty through meetings and workshops in which study abroad and complementary

      curricular issues and questions can be discussed and
      explored.

5. Bring to the attention of our college committee on
     educational policy these meetings and recommendations
     for their further consideration and implementation.

In general, the Study Abroad Articulation Project should prove to be a catalyst for concerted action that has long been thought of at the college but not yet taken. It has given us an incentive to plan a deeper, wider probe into curricular issues that, if not exactly overlooked, have not been adequately handled for the best interests of our students (and faculty) who are increasingly aware of a proliferation of opportunities abroad during the 10undergraduate years and the need for global literacy for every graduate.

Lastly, we want to acknowledge that the Study Abroad Articulation Project has brought together academic colleagues from various disciplines, pursuing common interests and questions, and we look forward to a commitment to continue the investigations into productive educational goals and an enriched liberal arts curriculum.

10

INTERNATIONALIZING UNDERGRADUATE EDUCATION THROUGH STUDY ABROAD: ISSUES AND OUTLOOK

Barbara B. Burn

The Study Abroad Articulation Project concluded with a two-day workshop hosted by the University of Massachusetts at Amherst and organized by its International Programs Office. In order to analyze and share findings with more than the eight SAAP institutions, an additional eight were each invited to send two-person teams. The notion behind inviting two people rather than a single representative was so that at these institutions efforts to disseminate SAAP findings and to implement relevant recommendations coming out of the workshop would not depend upon a single individual. Also participating in the concluding workshop were the project consultants. All the institutions and individuals involved in the workshop are listed in Appendix I.

This final chapter on the Study Abroad Articulation Project draws heavily on the workshop presentations and discussions. In so doing it presents and synthesizes the major findings and views.

PRE-STUDY ABROAD NEEDS

If study abroad is to be an integral part of undergraduates' degree programs, various requirements, some quite obvious, must be met. Students must not only study abroad but must make plans to do so sufficiently far in advance so that at least some of the course work done abroad can be in the field of their major. Clearly, a prior condition for this is that students choose their majors early in their college career, preferably during the freshman year.

Pre-study abroad needs also relate to what Richard D. Lambert, one of the SAAP consultants, refers to as "enclaving" which he has describes as follows: "One of the general problems facing study... is that except for foreign language majors it is by and large a totally enclaved experience. That is, it has little to do with anything else the student does on the home campus... most students take very little course work specifically aimed at preparing them for study abroad."

For study abroad to contribute to the internationalization of students' home campus programs, it should not be an isolated or "enclaved" experience. Students' pre-study abroad period should relate to and help prepare students for the academic learning in the study abroad country.

Models for this among the SAAP case studies include Georgetown University's new pre-study abroad course that highlights some major differences between the higher education systems of the United States and continental Europe. After all, how can students be expected to do serious work abroad in their majors when the home and host country higher education systems digress so much? The Georgetown course helps prepare students for such differences as professors' inaccessibility to students and lack of office hours, and their expectations of student performance, the availability of library resources, academic advising, and other study resources and support, and the kind of intellectual challenge likely—or not likely—in the foreign study experience. At the University of Massachusetts at Amherst, a weekly series of non-credit seminar discussion sessions offered to undergraduates the spring semester before their academic year at a British university helps prepare them for the academic and cross-cultural experience ahead. Both the Georgetown and UM/A programs in somewhat parallel ways equip students effectively to handle systems and cultural differences as they pursue studies abroad in their major.

Notable among efforts to relate pre-study abroad and study abroad learning are Kalamazoo College's extended pre-study abroad programs in which students participate the summer prior to their two to three quarters abroad. The "bridge activities" at Earlham College offer still another model in linking pre- and post-study abroad with learning while abroad. Students before going abroad are encouraged to consult with a faculty members whose course they expect to take on returning to Earlham in order to define for the student an activity abroad that can have a meaningful application in that course.

Earlham's bridging activities, while not necessarily involving students' studies in their major, suggest another important pre-study abroad need. For students to have course work done abroad count toward and be part of their studies for their major, their faculty advisers for the major have to approve this. To do so these faculty need adequate information on the courses their advisees plan to take while abroad.

CURRICULAR CONSTRAINTS AND OPPORTUNITIES

Curricular and related constraints can discourage if not prohibit undergraduates from taking courses abroad in their major.   While this applies especially to the sciences and professional fields, one finds it in the social sciences and even the humanities as well. In engineering, for example, the number and rigid sequencing of courses required for the major, together with the problem of recognizing courses offered elsewhere as equivalent to some of the required courses at the home campus, can result in the prolongation of the time period required to earn the degree.

Another kind of curricular situation that can discourage study abroad, not just in the major, but in general, may be course scheduling at the home institution that allows some courses only to be offered every other semester, or more likely, every other year.   As was found with Pomona College, this can be an important deterrent to study abroad for students needing to take such courses at the home campus. In this situation students are unable to include study abroad in their undergraduate career, let alone integrate it into the major.

All too often much more attention is devoted to why undergraduates should not study abroad and what kinds of courses they should not enroll in while abroad than to the exciting curricular opportunities it can open at home and abroad and how these can be integrated into and internationalize students' total degree programs.   The Study Abroad Articulation Project and its concluding workshop suggested several models.

The University of Colorado at Boulder tied in the study abroad experience of students majoring in international relations through its SAAP-supported project under which faculty involved in the interdepartmental major identified goals for the study abroad period of IR majors. This enabled both the students and the faculty to become more aware of and strengthen its connection with IR majors' studies at Boulder. It also responded to the recent demand of the state legislature that the university assess/identify the outcomes of educational programs.

The "bridge activities" developed by Earlham made of its students' study abroad experience an opportunity to shape curricula so as to take advantage of and build on that experience. A feature common to the Georgetown and Earlham models comprised faculty workshops to encourage and support the curricular innovations initiated by both institutions as part of their strategy of internationalizing their curricula by "curricularizing the international."

A new program at Lewis and Clark College, one of the non-SAAP institutions invited to our Amherst workshop, links overseas study with the core curriculum. The new Lewis and Clark "International Education/Core Linkage Project" enables undergraduates to fulfill various core curriculum requirements while studying abroad, especially certain "inquiry" courses and a writing requirement. At the same time this improves the quality of the study abroad experience, enhances students' field research skills, and adds to the internationalization of education at Lewis and Clark.

Another curricular opportunity made possible by study abroad is to encourage and institutionalize undergraduates' fulfilling part of the home campus language requirement through study abroad. For example, students from institutions with a two-year requirement should be able to do the equivalent of the second year through a semester of intensive study in a program abroad. This is encouraged at UM/A because of the dramatic strides possible in the language and also the cultural immersion offered by the program.

As these few illustrations suggest, students' taking courses abroad can widen and strengthen the academic offerings of U.S. colleges and universities. Too often, however, study abroad is perceived as a possible threat to the quality of the home campus degree or to enrollments, with quite different kinds of institutions having one or another of these concerns. The former tend to come from among -- but to constitute only a small fraction of the highly selective colleges and universities. The former institutions doubt that the academic quality of other institutions, whether foreign or American, can measure up to their standards. The latter institutions tend to be less selective and more enrollment-driven, concerned to keep their dormitories and classrooms filled.

RETURNEES

The SAEP found that many study abroad returnees have a feeling of alienation back at their home campus. Many found it difficult to identify courses that built on or took advantage of students' study abroad learning. At some campuses faculty tended to view the course work students did abroad as peripheral to rather than an important part of their major program. Rarely is the academic learning achieved through study abroad deliberately woven into students' home campus academic programs. Typically, little effort is made to ease or even note returnees' possible problems of reentry or reintegration. Several SAAP efforts targeted these gaps and negative features.

At Kalamazoo College a major concern was that study abroad returnees from foreign language countries may have little encouragement and opportunity to maintain, let alone add to, their foreign language proficiency, a proficiency that advanced dramatically while they were abroad. Kalamazoo investigators recommended that more faculty members, especially in fields where the literature is international, assign readings in foreign language sources to their students. In several departments at the University of Massachusetts, (e.g. in History and Psychology) student accomplishment abroad, especially in independent research, is now recognized as qualifying returnees to be honors students and/or undergraduate research and teaching assistants.

The Earlham College "bridges" project mentioned earlier may be more feasible at the smaller higher education institutions than at those with some thousands of students. However, in orchestrating a number of dimensions of higher eduction, it is an exciting if not widely applicable model. One of its main strengths is that rather than imposing additional requirements and expectations on students, it is essentially optional. Rather than subjecting study abroad to tests of value and skill acquisition, it offers students the opportunity to reflect on and therefore affect what their international experience does to their lives, and, more immediately, to their college careers. This approach was summarized by the SAAP coordinator at Earlham, Richard T. Jurasek, as follows: "The bridge activities must be modest in scope... We fail if it is perceived by the students as yet one more task to carry out rather than as a chance to gain new insights and make new connections that will lead to enhanced learning when the student returns to campus."

Under Georgetown's SAAP activity, study abroad returnees remain involved with their a foreign study experience. The GU/SAAP project was based on the assumption that students' study abroad experience should shape their senior year as well as defining the junior year and giving direction to the sophomore year. In meeting these aims, study abroad would internationalize students' study programs at GU as well as abroad. The new program at Lewis and Clark should reduce the alienation of study abroad returnees by linking the sophomore, junior, and senior years through sequenced courses focused on international learning. In its first year, 1989-1990, the returnees took courses that integrated their international experience under such rubrics as gender, sex, religion, and developing world issues. The Lewis and Clark program represents a comprehensive and ambitious model not just to internationalize study abroad students' degree programs but to internationalize curricula at the institution.

THE ROLE OF THE FACULTY

While findings of the University of California Study Abroad Articulation Project do not, of course, reflect the attitudes of faculty members nationally toward study abroad, certainly the ignorance, indifference, and often negative attitude of academics towards study abroad is a major impediment to its being integrated into students' degree programs. In the Study Abroad Evaluation Project it was the lack of encouragement by faculty for students to study abroad that was an especially important deterrent! The UC faculty survey showed that faculty members to a considerable extent prefer that students not do course work abroad in their major and that the question of the quality of academic offerings at foreign universities was a concern, more so for faculty in the sciences than in the humanities and social sciences. The following statement of UC findings suggests the dimensions of the problem: "Fifty-eight point eight percent of the respondents considered the contribution to students' major programs to be only minor; 23.1 % considered the contribution to general academic development to be minor, and 26.8 % considered the contribution to career or further educational opportunities to be minor."

The requirements that faculty members impose on students majoring in their departments involve another aspect of the faculty role in study abroad. It is common for departments to require their majors to take certain specified courses or a certain number of courses toward the major in the department. This has to do with various factors: faculty concern that the students' programs adequately prepare them in terms of the state of the discipline, the view that certain courses should be required both for preparatory and winnowing purposes, faculty reluctance to see students earn their degree from their department when the students have done much of the work for their major elsewhere, and, in some more enrollment-driven institutions, concern to keep students at the home campus. Even at colleges and universities without such bureaucratic and related requirements, faculty members may discourage study abroad in the major so that students do not complete much of the course work for their major abroad but as returnees take courses in the department. Its program is then enriched and, indeed, internationalized by the students' international experience and learning.

Much more attention should be accorded to the question of why should faculty encourage study abroad. As suggested, there are plenty of reasons why they might not wish to do so. In response to this question, it is well documented that students who have been abroad make an enormous difference in their courses on their return, for example, in classroom discussion and in the subjects they choose for required papers. Their greatly enhanced concern for international issues also helps to internationalize extracurricular activities at their institutions.

In the SAAP workshop discussions of the role of faculty, among aspects debated were the faculty reward systems (promotion and tenure), whether the ambience of particular institutions is propitious to the promoting of international experience, and the impact of the relative emphasis placed at a given institution on teaching and advising on the one hand and on research and publication on the other. It was agreed that at the highly research-oriented institutions, faculty members' spending time in advising students on study abroad or initiating new study abroad arrangements or themselves teaching abroad as part of interinstitutional international collaboration is not apt to count much towards tenure or promotion. These activities are much more likely to be counted at the smaller liberal arts colleges where teaching is prized, student advising is rewarded, and institutional leadership strongly supports international education. Looked at from these perspectives, study abroad is not apt to become a significant priority with faculty members at U.S. colleges and universities unless the strong leadership of an individual institution mandates it, or until there is much wider public recognition of the importance of international education to the performance of the United States in more and more critical fields.

ISSUES FOR THE FUTURE

If study abroad is to articulate more effectively with students' home campus programs and help internationalize them by being more integrated into them, the eight-institution Study Abroad Articulation Project has revealed major dimensions of this challenge. The institutional, program, and student surveys, the faculty seminars and consultations, the discussions held among SAAP institutional coordinators two to three times a year during the period of the project, and the final workshop made clear that this articulation and integration depend on efforts in many directions and at several levels.

At the most practical level, among important needs are early planning by students and the availability of adequate information on study abroad opportunities for them. This information should be in the institution's course catalog, faculty/staff advising handbooks, departmental publications that describe options and requirements for majors, and publications given to prospective students and new faculty and staff. These information needs make ongoing communication with faculty about study abroad a sine qua non for effective articulation. Other practical needs for better articulation involve the timing of and time period for study abroad, as illustrated by the Pomona College experience.

For faculty members to be more supportive of study abroad as an integral part of their students' programs, they need to know and approve the substance and content as well as the quality of course work their students do abroad. More basic, they must accept the possibility that students majoring in their department can earn their institution's degree even though some of their course work for the major is done elsewhere. Many colleges and universities in the United States are ambivalent about this. While some have no problem with it, others maintain a relatively rigid expectation that their students do their work for their major at the home campus.

It is ironic that the new European Community (EC) student exchange program, ERASMUS (Expanded Regional Action Scheme for the Mobility of University Students), is catalyzing so much study abroad (within the EC) even though for the most part the EC countries have no system for academic credit transfer, while the

United States, though having such a system, lags in serious and integrated study abroad. It is also ironic that an increasing number of American students in the professional fields are choosing to study abroad in the conviction that the experience will enhance their job qualifications, and yet, as just mentioned, many U.S. faculty discourage American students from doing course work in their major while studying abroad. Instead they are urged to use their electives, a situation that reflects and reenforces the relatively low priority often accorded to the role of elective courses in undergraduate education at many U.S. colleges and universities.

It must also be admitted, however, that not many U.S. students are capable of doing course work in their major while studying abroad if they go to a foreign language country. One therefore finds that whereas EC students in engineering, business, law, and the like are studying in these specializations in another EC country and in its language, American students studying in France, Germany, or other continental European countries are either taking courses offered in English by home-campus or other English-speaking teachers or are studying the host country's language and culture. If greater articulation and integration are to be achieved between home campus and foreign studies, American students' proficiency in foreign languages must be dramatically improved.

Finally, for American colleges and universities to integrate study abroad into their degree programs as a way of internationalizing them, a key would be to give recognition in the faculty reward system for the contribution of faculty members to study abroad. Only then would faculty be motivated to implement this as an institutional and professional priority. At present faculty contributions to study abroad tend not to rank high at the more selective and elite institutions, for example, advising students about study abroad, serving as a program director, or participating in campus committees relating to study abroad and international education. Added to this, faculty members who have a chance for travel abroad in connection with their institution's international education programs may be perceived and resented by their colleagues as having a special advantage or opportunity that is reward enough in itself! In connection with the need for faculty support of study abroad, an important feature of the ERASMUS program is that all student exchanges under it depend on faculty members at collaborating institutions for their initiation and implementation.

If the participation of American undergraduates in study abroad grows significantly, and international experience becomes more common for undergraduates, some colleges and universities may claim that in encouraging and facilitating undergraduate study abroad, they have demonstrated adequate commitment to international education. However, as some of the SAAP case studies show, for study abroad to be a significant part of students' education, it needs to link into and shape the "before and after" at their home campus. In short, higher education institutions should not consider that they have acquitted their responsibilities for international education simply by encouraging and enabling it to happen in a foreign country, not at the home campus.

The preceding comments may have focused unduly on obstacles and issues that impede foreign study integration into undergraduates' college careers. The diversity of higher education institutions in the United States makes it impossible to make generalizations, whether about study abroad or other topics, that are widely valid. An increasing number of American colleges and universities are or have been giving priority to international education, including study abroad, especially such undergraduate-oriented liberal arts colleges as Earlham, Lewis and Clark, Pomona, and Kalamazoo. For institutions wishing to go more in this direction, many positive models exist.

The longer-range outlook for internationalizing American education by making study abroad a more integral part of it and for more students in more fields is excellent. International interdependence with its accompanying tensions and opportunities puts a premium on international education. Study abroad attracts an increasing number of students, including those in professional fields, so that more and more colleges and universities are in fact highlighting their offerings in this area as a student recruitment strategy. The model and achievements of ERASMUS in the EC countries on the one hand, and the impressive and accelerating involvement in and commitment to student exchanges of institutions in Japan on the other hand, make it unthinkable that American higher education will not make study abroad and international exchanges a more important priority. In so doing U.S. colleges and universities should also come to grips with the question of how American students who for various reasons do not study abroad can, at their home institutions, have an international education experience that is also motivating and educational throughout their lives.

NOTE
1. The U.S. involvement in the SAEP is reported in Jerry Carlson, Barbara B. Burn, John Useem, and David Yachimowicz, *Study Abroad: The Experience of American Undergraduates* (Westport, Conn.: Greenwood Press, 1990).

APPENDIX: PARTICIPANTS IN THE PROJECT, PROJECT CONSULTANTS AND OTHER WORKSHOP PARTICIPANTS

UNIVERSITY OF MASSACHUSETTS AT AMHERST
Barbara B. Burn, Associate Provost, International Programs, and Project Coordinator
Maryelise S. Lamet, Associate Director, International Programs
Carol J. Lebold, Assistant Study Abroad Coordinator
EARLHAM COLLEGE
Richard T. Jurasek, Professor, Department of Languages
GEORGETOWN UNIVERSITY
William W. Cressey, Director, International Programs
UNIVERSITY OF CALIFORNIA AT RIVERSIDE
Jerry S. Carlson, Professor, Department of Psychology
Theda Shapiro, Professor, Department of Literature and Languages
UNIVERSITY OF COLORADO, BOULDER
Jean Delaney, Director of International Education
KALAMAZOO COLLEGE
Joe K. Fugate, Director of Foreign Study
POMONA COLLEGE
Cecilia Cloughly, Director, Office of International Education
SMITH COLLEGE
Robert C. Davis, Professor, Department of German
Patricia C. Olmstead, Associate Dean for Intercollegiate Study

ADDITIONAL PARTICIPANTS IN CONCLUDING WORKSHOP
BROWN UNIVERSITY
Duncan Smith, Dean, International Programs & Exchanges
Gisela Belton, Associate Director, International Programs & Exchanges
UNIVERSITY OF COLORADO, BOULDER
Lou McClelland, Director of Research & Testing
HOPE COLLEGE
Neal Sobania, Director, International Education
Jon Huisken, Registrar

UNIVERSITY OF ILLINOIS
Joan Solaun, Director, Study Abroad
Joanne Reska, Associate Director, Study Abroad
KALAMAZOO COLLEGE
Joseph Brockington, Associate Professor, Department of German
LEWIS & CLARK UNIVERSITY
R. Vance Savage, Dean, International Education
Steven Knox, Profess or of English
MOUNT HOLYOKE COLLEGE
Joanne Picard, Dean of International Affairs
David Ellison, Professor of French
PENNSYLVANIA STATE UNIVERSITY
Elizabeth Smith, Profess of Art History; Academic Officer
Kirsten Moritz, Coordinator of Academic Services
POMONA COLLEGE
Margaret Dornish, Professor, Department of Religion
SAINT OLAF COLLEGE
Sue Clark, Director, International Studies
Lee Swan, Associate Dean, International Studies
Robert Nichols, Professor of History
WELLESLEY COLLEGE
Barbara Brown, Foreign Student Adviser

PROJECT CONSULTANTS
Elinor G. Barber, Director, Research Division, Institute of
International Education
Richard D. Lambert, Director, National Foreign Language Center
John Useem, Professor Emeritus, Department of Sociology,
Michigan State University

REFERENCES

Abrams, I. (1960) *Study Abroad. New dimensions in higher education: some newer developments.* New York: McGraw-Hill.

Bachner, D.J. & Zeutschel, U. (1990), *Students of four decades.* Washington, D.C.: Youth for Understanding.

Barrow, T., Ager, S.M., Bennett, M.F., Brown, H.I., Clark, J.D.L., Harris, L.G., & Klein, S.F. (1981). *College students' knowledge and beliefs: A survey of global understanding.* New Rochelle, NY: Change Magazine Press.

Burn, B.B. (1990). *The contribution of international educational exchange to the international education of Americans*: projections for the year 2000. Occasional Papers 26, Forum Series. New York: Council on International Education Exchange.

Burn B.B. (1980). *Expanding the international dimensions of higher education.* San Francisco: Jossey-Bass.

Burn, B.B. (1985). Higher education is international. In W.H. Allaway & H.C.Shorrock (Eds.), *Dimensions of international higher education.* Boulder, CO: Westview.

Burn, B.B. & Briggs, A. (1985). *Study abroad: A European and American perspective on organization and impact of study abroad.* Amsterdam: European Institute of Education and Policy Study.

Burn, B.B.. Cerych, C. & Smith, A. (Ed.). (1990). *Study Abroad Programmes.* London: Jessica Kingsley Publishers.

Carlson, J.S., Burn, B.B., Useem, J. & Yachimowicz, D. (1990). *Study abroad: the experience of American undergraduates.* Westport, CT: Greenwood Press.

Carlson, J.S. & Widaman, K.F. (1988). The effects of study abroad during college on attitudes toward other cultures. *International Journal of Intercultural Relations,* 12, 1-17.

Carlson, J.S. & Yachimowicz, D. (1986). *Evaluation of the University of California's Education Abroad Program: The 1985-86 Participant Questionnaire.* Santa Barbara: University of California.

Carlson, J.S. & Yachimowicz, D. (1987). *Evaluation of the University of California's Education Abroad Program: The 1986-87 Participant Questionnaire.* Santa Barbara: The University of California.

Carsello, C. & Greiser, J. (1976). How college students change during study abroad. *College Student Journal,* 10, 276-278.

Church, A.T. (1982). Sojourner adjustment. *Psychological Bulletin*, 91, 540-572.

Coelho, M. (1962). Personal growth and educational development through working and studying abroad. *Journal of Social Issues*, 18, 55-67.

German Academic Exchange Service (DAAD). (1980). *Research on exchanges: Proceeding of the German-American conference at the Wissenschaftszentrum*. Bonn: DAAD.

Goodwin, C. & Nacht, M. (1988). *Abroad and beyond*. New York: Cambridge University Press.

Hull, F. (1978). *Foreign students in the United States of America: Coping behavior within the education environment*. New York: Praeger.

Jusasek, R. (1988). Integrating foreign languages into the college curriculum. *The Modern Language Journal*, 72, 52-58

Klineberg, O. (1981). The role of international university exchanges. In S. Bochner (Ed.), *The mediating person*. Cambridge, MA: Shenkman.

Koester, J. (1985). *A profile of the U.S. student abroad*. New York: Council on International Educational Exchange.

Koester, J. (1987). *A profile of the U.S. student abroad—1984-85*. New York: Council on International Educational Exchange.

Lambert, R.D. (1989). *International studies and the undergraduate*. Washington, DC: American Council on Education.

Lamet, S.A. & Lamet, M.S. (1981). The impact of international exchanges on university students. *International Understanding at School*, 41, 7-8.

Markovits, A.S. & Keeler, J.T.S. (1978). The Euro-consciousness of American college students: a survey of knowledge and attitudes at five "elite" institutions. *European Studies Newsletter*, 7, 1-24.

Melchiori, A. & Slind, M.G. (1987). *Relationships of Undergraduate Study Abroad and Subsequent Academic Performance*. Unpublished paper (Washington State University).

National Task Force on Undergraduate Education Abroad (1990). *A national mandate for education abroad: getting with the task.*. Washington, DC: National Association for Foreign Student Affairs.

Office for Cooperation in Education (1985). *Study abroad in the European Community*. Brussels: European Institute of Education and Social Policy.

Opper, S., Teichler, U. & Carlson, J.S. (1990). *Impacts of Study abroad Programmes on Students and Graduates*. London: Jessica Kingsley Publishers.

President's Commission on Foreign Language and International Studies. (1980a). *A report to the president from the President's Commission*. Washington, DC: Government Printing Office.

President's Commission on Foreign Language and International Studies. (1980b). *Background papers and studies*. Washington, DC: Government Printing Office.

Sanders, I.T. & Ward, J.C. (1970). *Bridges to understanding: International programs of American colleges and universities*. New York: McGraw-Hill.

Sell, D.K. (1983). Attitude change in foreign study participants. *International Journal of Intercultural Relations, 7*, 131-147.

Stassen, M. (1985). Objective and cognitive dimensions of study abroad. In W.H. Allaway & H.C. Shorrock (Eds.), *Dimensions of international higher education*. Boulder, CO: Westview.

Weaver, H., Martin, J., Burn, B.B., Useem, J., & Carlson, J.S. (1987). *A researcher's guide to international educational exchange*. Santa Barbara: University of California.

Yachimowicz, D.J. (1987). "The effect of study abroad during college on international understanding and attitudes toward the homeland and other cultures." Doctoral dissertation, University of California, Riverside.

INDEX

Questionnaire(s): on fulfillment
    of major requirements,
    100-104; on non-
    participation in study
    abroad, 73-74, 75-83, 88-
    90; in SAEP study, 2

Reintegration: application of
    language skills and, 16-
    18, 38-42, 116;
    discussion groups and,
    18-21; "reentry course"
    and, 60; research
    projects and, 21-22;
    SAAP findings on, 128-
    29; SAEP results on, 5-6.
    See also Post-sojourn
    period; Returnees
Required course work. See
    General education
    requirements; Major
    requirements
Research projects, 21-22
Retention rate, 45-46
Returnees: as in-class "experts,"
    20-21; long-term impact
    of sojourn on, 53-54;
    SAAP findings on, 128-
    29; sense of alienation
    and, 20, 48, 129. See
    also Post-sojourn
    period; Reintegration

Safety concerns, 82
Scholarships, 84
Science majors, 46, 74-75, 76,
    79, 81. See also
    Professional programs
Sheirich, Richard, 87
Skill development abroad, 8.
    See also Foreign
    language skill; Major
    requirements
Smith College, 109-23;
    administration of study

abroad programs at,
    112-13; Associated
    Kyoto Program (AKP) at,
    117, 121; Committee on
    Study Abroad, 112;
    German case study at,
    117-19; history of
    international education
    at, 109-12; Japanese
    case study at, 119-22;
    language-based vs.
    international studies-
    based programs at, 110;
    pre- and post-sojourn
    language study at, 113-
    17; recommendations
    from SAAP study, 122-
    23
Social issues, 11, 62
Social science majors, 15-22, 46,
    74-75, 76
Sojourn period abroad: course
    load during, 46-47;
    duration of, 86;
    integration into host
    country life and, 5, 31,
    35; learning
    accomplished during, 7-
    9, 57; refinement of
    language skills during,
    35-38; SAEP results on,
    4-6; timing of, 71, 72,
    84-85, 101-2, 131
Study Abroad Evaluation
    Project (SAEP):
    participating
    institutions, 1;
    questionnaires in, 2;
    research design for, 1-2;
    research questions in, 1;
    results from, 1-6, 128
Study abroad programs:
    attitudes of faculty
    members toward, 49-51,
    101-4, 110-11, 112, 129;